A PIONEER IN MADAGASCAR

JOSEPH PEARSE

Yours affectionately,
J. Pearse.

A Pioneer in Madagascar

JOSEPH PEARSE

OF THE L.M.S.

BY

C. F. A. MOSS, M.D.
TANANARIVE, MADAGASCAR

ILLUSTRATED

NEGRO UNIVERSITIES PRESS
NEW YORK

BV
3625
. M22
P4
1969

Originally published in 1913
by Headley Brothers, London

Reprinted 1969 by
Negro Universities Press
A Division of Greenwood Press, Inc.
New York

SBN 8371-2781-5

PREFACE

MR. PEARSE was one of the second band of missionaries sent to Madagascar after the reopening of the island to mission work. His term of service extended over forty-one years. During that time immense changes came over the native church and his contributions thereto were of no mean order. It so happens that he was the first London Missionary Society missionary of long standing in the island to pass away. The length of his own service, the strenuous nature of his work, much of it of a pioneer character, and the very high esteem in which he was held, all appeared to justify the attempt to produce some memorial of him. From letters, reports, diaries and magazine articles a large amount of material was forthcoming, which has been freely used in the preparation of these pages.

Grateful acknowledgment must be made of valuable help rendered by many, especially Rev. R. Wardlaw Thompson, D.D., for permission to use the material at the London Mission House; Rev. J. Sibree, F.R.G.S., for permission to quote from the "Antanànarìvo Annual," as well as for his own recollections; Mr. Henry Card, of Lewes, for the loan of an unbroken collection of letters extending over fifty-three years; Rev. Charles Jukes, for kindly revising the manuscript, and several members of

Mr. Pearse's family for very great assistance of a similar character; also Messrs. James Clarke and Co. for permission to use a paper in the *Christian World*; Mr. John Parrett for the use of photographs, and Mr. Swan Watson, of Edinburgh, for the portraits. Our thanks must also be accorded to many in Madagascar, both of the missionaries and of the natives, who have written most interesting and valuable appreciations of Mr. Pearse and his work.

C. F. A. Moss.

Buckhurst Hill,
   March, 1913.

CONTENTS

vii

viii   Contents

Contents

LIST OF ILLUSTRATIONS

FOREWORD

EVERY great Society has its specially romantic and
striking object lessons of the wonderful results which
have followed the proclamation of the Gospel among the
heathen and ignorant peoples. Madagascar has been
to the London Missionary Society one of these out-
standing monuments of the power and grace of God.
The early story of the introduction of Christianity
among the people is one of thrilling interest. The
long dark period of persecution, with its amazing results
in the diffusion of knowledge, the strengthening of faith
in the Word of God, and the increase in the number of
believers, is one of the miracles of grace in the Mission
Field, and the subsequent history of the Mission in the
early enthusiasm of new converts, the gathering in of
great multitudes to the confession of faith, and the
indications of life and growing character during the
long period of difficulty which supervened on the French
conquest, show that the Christian profession of the
Malagasy Church has not been a mere form. The
multitudes of truly converted men and women who are
growing in the grace and knowledge of Jesus Christ have
made this Mission an object of profound interest and of
deep thanksgiving to God.

Such Missions owe much to the men who are among

their pioneers, though it may also be truly said that they
have a wonderful power of making men. The conditions
in which men find themselves speedily bring out all the
latent power and the unsuspected gifts of those who are
sent out as missionaries. This was conspicuously the
case with the subject of the following memoir. As a
youth and as a student for the ministry he was quiet,
contemplative, but not conspicuous. He went out to
Madagascar stirred in heart by the news which came of
the death of the persecuting Queen, and the opening of
the country to Missions, and by the appeal for men to
go and teach the large company of ignorant people who
were professing themselves on the side of Christ. Every
year of his long term of service in the island proved more
conclusively his exceptional gifts and beautiful consecration. There has certainly been no man in the
Mission who has more thoroughly deserved to have his
life-story told.

Mr. Pearse had a very varied and, in some parts of it, a
very trying experience of missionary life. After some
years of earnest and untiring labour in the Capital,
building up a large Church at Anàlakèly, and effectively
helping in the establishment of a second Church at
Fàravòhitra, he and his devoted wife volunteered for
pioneer work among the semi-barbarous Sihànaka
tribes, a week's journey to the north of the capital.
Notwithstanding the little-concealed hostility of the
people to the Hovas and all who came from them,
notwithstanding their inveterate drinking habits and the
fever-saturated climate of the Antsihànaka country,

Mr. and Mrs. Pearse, with splendid heroism and self-abnegation, succeeded in doing a fine work, though at serious cost to their own health. After some years, difficulties having arisen in the Mission to the south of the Capital in the Bètsilèo country, which required the exercise of great wisdom and tact and grace to settle them, Mr. Pearse was selected by the Directors, with the approval of his colleagues, as the man best suited for the task, and sent down to Fìanàrantsòa, and the choice was abundantly justified by the result.

Mr. Pearse was an all-round missionary who seemed to be equally good in very different branches of work. He had acquired by study and practice a considerable knowledge of medicine, and was very successful in his use of it. He had given himself to the study of the native language, with such effect that the people claimed him as no longer a European but one of themselves, because he spoke in such an absolutely free and idiomatic fashion.

As a preacher and speaker he was greatly appreciated everywhere. The books he prepared for the use of the Malagasy were, and are still, highly prized ; and, above all, his personal influence, due to great tactfulness, combined with a very devout and prayerful spirit, was in times of difficulty invaluable.

Dr. Moss has done well in gathering up the facts of this noble life, and his simple narrative, with the large space given to Mr. Pearse's own record of his experiences and impressions, cannot fail to interest a wide circle. He was worthy for whom this modest monument is prepared.

R. WARDLAW THOMPSON.

NOTE
ON THE PRONUNCIATION OF MALAGASY NAMES

Malagasy names often seem exceedingly long, but their pronunciation is quite easy. Every letter is pronounced. The vowels are pronounced pretty much as follows :

> a is like ah or the a in father.
> e is like a in mate.
> i is like ee in meet.
> o is like oo in moon.
> ao is pronounced like o in John.
> ai is pronounced like i in write.

The accentuation of the syllables is of great importance and those which are accented have been indicated in the text.

CHAPTER I

Early Years

1837 to 1863

ON the 27th November, 1837, Joseph Pearse was born, the eldest son and third child in a family of twelve. His parents were simple, devout people, residing at that time at Islington, but later removing to the charming village of Brockham in Surrey. The father was a commercial traveller, a good man, highly trusted, and a very hard worker; the mother, loving and careful, and an excellent manager.

Of Mr. Pearse's early development and history it is impossible now to obtain any details. Those who knew him then have all passed away, and to friends of later years, as well as to the younger members of his family, he appeared with his character already determined and his inclinations already directed towards a serious purpose. His bent was more towards reading than towards games, and he was fond, as a boy, of exercising himself in English composition during his leisure times.

He has himself preserved in an old diary a few facts of interest, which shall be forthwith quoted :—

"Until May 21st, 1852, I remained at home, except for a short time when I went to a boarding school at Hythe. On that, to me, ever-memorable day I left home to enter upon a term of apprenticeship at a retail draper's at Lewes. From that day I date my first religious impressions : I was deeply affected at leaving home, and, after I had bidden farewell to my beloved parents and sisters, I felt my need of true and abiding happiness, and was led to seek it, where alone it is to be found. Of the time I spent at Lewes I have the most pleasant recollections. I was very happy there and was surrounded by many kind Christian friends. I joined the Church assembling at the ' Tabernacle,' under the pastoral care of the Rev. E. Jones. After staying a little more than five years, I left and took a situation at Messrs. Cook's in St. Paul's Churchyard. I soon joined the Church at the Poultry under Dr. Spence. I had long had the desire to devote myself to the work of the Lord, but hitherto the way had not been open for me. After having been in London, however, about two years, Dr. Spence proposed that I should make application to New College ; I consented and was accepted.

" Of that Institution I have been a member up to within a few weeks of this time. I have now left, having on February 9th been accepted by the London Missionary Society, as a missionary to Madagascar. To-morrow (May 20th, 1863) I am publicly set apart for the work of the Lord, and sensible as I am of the many imperfections of my past life, I would desire to make a fresh start on the solemn occasion. I would ' forget the past,' and by the grace of God I solemnly resolve ' Henceforth to live.' "

During the time of his residence in Lewes it is clear that he awoke to the privileges of Christian communion with others, and to the duty of working for the spread of Christ's kingdom, according to his opportunity. He left the Anglican communion at this time. He found work to do in the Sunday School, and there are still

extant letters, received by him from some of his scholars
in whose spiritual condition he was deeply interested.
To some of these he wrote, even after leaving Lewes,
words of entreaty, warning and encouragement. He
himself ever gratefully acknowledged the helpful friendship at that time of Mr. Card, the Superintendent of
the Sunday School, with whom he corresponded, with
more or less regularity, throughout the whole of his life,
and who has lovingly kept all the letters he had received,
from 1857 up till the close of 1910.

That the question of his life work was seriously
engaging his attention is shown by a long letter to his
mother, dated December 14th, 1854, in which he says :
" I have been thinking about what I was to do, after I
had faithfully served my apprenticeship here. I desired,
if I could see my way clear, to devote my life entirely
to the service of Him, who hath called me out of darkness into His marvellous light. I wanted, as I thought,
to be a minister of the Gospel that I might more publicly
go forth and proclaim to others the preciousness of
Christ my Saviour." He proceeds to enlarge upon the
steps he then took with a view to entering a College,
alluding incidentally to the advice of his master, who
had already signified his high opinion of the young
apprentice, by the gift of a silver watch, and who now
sought to dissuade him from so madly relinquishing a
life of such promise, regarded from a business point of
view. It was not this advice that interfered with the
consummation of his wishes at that time, but the sense
of his responsibility, as the eldest son, to be prepared
to contribute to the support of the family, in the event
of the death of his father. It was not until he had left
Lewes for London and become a member of Dr. Spence's
Church that the decision was eventually taken to

become a student for the ministry. His application to New College was favourably received, and he commenced his course there in January 1860. Of this step he writes to Mr. Card : " Unspeakable privilege ! For truly I may adopt the language of the apostle, and say, ' Unto me who am less than the least of all saints is this grace given that I should preach among the Gentiles the un- searchable riches of Christ.' Immense responsibility ! To be the ambassador of Christ, to fit souls for Eternity, to minister the things of God, ' Who is sufficient for these things ? ' "

Soon after commencing his college course he wrote again to the same friend and such sentences as the following indicate the trend of his thoughts at the time : " At present I am principally engaged with languages, and get but little that you would suppose was necessary to fit me for the sacred office of the ministry, but that I shall receive in due course. The influence of close application upon the mind is not to increase spiritual life. Oh, Sir ! if you value, as I feel you do, an earnest evangelical ministry, pray much for students. . . . . Let us look long and often at the face of the Crucified One, and then we shall feel the little flame of love burning in our own hearts, which shall exert a mighty power on our own lives and which, by the help of God, shall enable us to exert an influence over others."

The half century which has elapsed since those student days has been bridged over by the kindness of two honoured fellow students, who have written their recollections. The Rev. J. Alden Davies writes : " I am unable to say anything about Mr. Pearse's progress in technical scholarship, which I believe was entirely respectable ; but can simply speak of the impression he made in the outer circle of college life. A remarkably handsome man, obviously earnest, serious and stedfast ; a good man, endowed with much emotional power. His services were greatly valued at our village chapels and elsewhere ; his sermons were matter of deep devotional purpose with him, even to tears. I called upon him now and then, and he, more rarely, on me ; sometimes we had tea together and occasionally worked together at our Hebrew. I remember very distinctly the interest that was taken in his approaching departure ; and that I with some others went down to the West India Docks, to bid him farewell in his cabin."

The Rev. Dr. Rowland writes : " He never attempted university examinations, nor did he appear to care much for such distinctions as might be gained thereby nor for the learning indicated by them. His heart was set on evangelistic work from the first, and the passion for souls, which made him so successful a missionary, revealed itself even in those early days. He was characterized at college by seriousness and even solemnity of manner, and took no part in the fun which often asserts itself among students ; indeed, to levity, his presence was often a silent rebuke. He was very simple-minded and single-hearted, so that he was by no means unpopular, in spite of a certain aloofness of manner, as of one conscious that he was set apart for a special and solemn work. He was greatly beloved in the village churches we were called upon to ' supply', for he excelled the rest of us in the simplicity and directness of his preaching and availed himself of every opportunity of doing pastoral work among the villagers. As a student it might have been said of him ' he was a good man, full of the Holy Ghost.' "

He has treasured, among his papers, letters from some

of the villagers, to whom his preaching had been a means
of good, especially in the little village of Burnham,
Bucks ; there are letters written in illiterate style, and
yet full of fervour and of grateful appreciation of his
instrumentality in the conversion of their writers.

One or two brief extracts from the replies made by
him at his ordination service will suffice to show his
own personal acceptance of the Christian faith, and of
the mission to which he was then being set apart : " That
I am a child of God I conclude from the change which
has taken place in my thoughts, words and conduct,
and from the one settled purpose of my mind, which is
to walk with God, to obey His precepts and to glorify
that Saviour, in whom alone I trust for salvation. . .
Those things which once I hated, now I love ; those
whom I once despised, I now delight to sojourn amongst ;
those services which were once the most irksome, I now
perform with the greatest joy ; of that Saviour whom I
once despised and rejected I can say that He is precious
to me, that I desire to walk in His footsteps, to imitate
His example and to spend myself and be spent in telling
of Him and His Salvation to my fellow creatures. . . .
My first desires after I had found the Saviour
myself were to carry the glad tidings of Him to the
heathen. . . . I trust to be enabled to ' preach the
word,' to be ' instant in season ' and out of season, to
reprove, rebuke, and exhort with all long suffering, to
make full proof of my ministry ' and to abide faithful,
even unto death.' . . . With a deep consciousness
of my own insufficiency, I cannot refrain from saying,
' Brethren, pray for me,' that when weak, the Lord's
power may be perfected in me, that when ignorant,
by Him I may be made wise, that though perplexed, I
may never despair, that though persecuted I may not

be forsaken, that when weary and faint I may be enabled to look to Jesus."

His ordination took place at the Poultry Chapel, and those who took part were Rev. J. S. Hall, Rev. G. Adeney, Rev. E. Prout, Rev. Dr. Spence and Rev. Dr. Halley. He had previously been married to Miss Mary Eyre Burn, of Chatham, and within a few days of these events, they bade farewell to their kin and set out for their distant home in Madagascar, and for the work to which they had devoted their lives.

CHAPTER II

Antanànarìvo and the Journey there

THE journey from London to Antanànarìvo was a very different matter in the year 1863, from what it is at the present time.

Then, the voyage was undertaken in a sailing vessel, which did not lose sight of England for perhaps a week, probably touched at no other port until her arrival at Mauritius about eighty-five days later, and on board of which the conditions were altogether different from those of to-day. Arrived at Mauritius, the traveller had still to tranship into a " bullocker," a small barque used for the traffic of bullocks between Madagascar and Mauritius, and, this very undesirable passage over, he and all his goods had to be conveyed to Antanànarìvo on the shoulders of native bearers, a journey lasting from eight to fifteen days.

Now, the journey is by steam-packet from Marseilles through the Suez Canal to Madagascar itself and occupies only twenty-one days and on arrival at the port of Tamatàve, a journey by steam-launch of one day, and by rail of another, will bring the traveller to Tanànarìve, under all the conditions of rush and hurry incidental to present-day travel.

Mr. Pearse, with his bride, joined a party of missionaries, who left London on 11th June, 1863, on the *Isabella Blyth*. Their fellow passengers were Mr. and

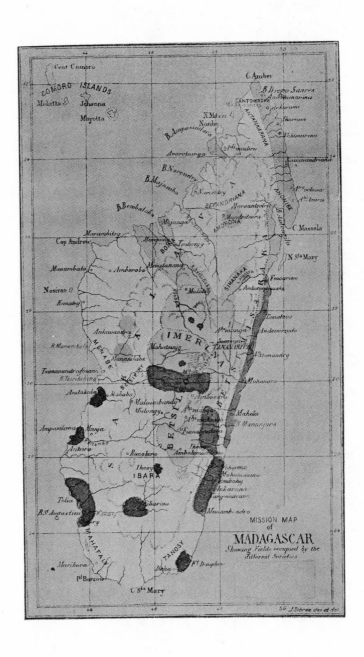

MISSION MAP
of
MADAGASCAR
Showing Fields occupied by the
different Societies

Mrs. Hartley, Mr. and Mrs. Kessler, and Mr. and Mrs. Briggs.

The voyage was evidently a pleasant one, but without variety, except in the matter of minute details, which the diary gratefully records. As soon as weather conditions permitted, the voyagers settled down to a daily routine which was subject to but little interruption. One entry in the diary fairly sums up the situation: " There is little around us or on board to interest us ; one day is almost a facsimile of another ; we read considerably and devote a fair time daily to the study of Malagasy."

His programme is indicated by a time table which says :

" Rise at 6 o'clock.
7 to 8 Malagasy Grammar.
9.30 to 12   ,,   ,,
12.30 to 3 Bible Study.
7 to 8 Reading.
8 to 9 Prayer."

This was a high ideal for shipboard, which he evidently found very difficult to carry out and he occasionally scolds himself in his diary for imperfect fulfilment of it. His orderly habit of mind delighted in rigid adherence to fixed times and was much tried by infractions of his self-imposed rules, which were quite inevitable, under the circumstances. Undoubtedly in this way lessons of consideration for others and accommodation to altered plans were learnt, which probably were more useful in the building up of his character, than a rigid adherence to a programme would have been. The missionaries met for worship in each other's cabins, and when the weather permitted, service was held on the deck on Sunday mornings.

The daily run varied from forty knots up to 217. At length, after experiencing storms, gales, heat and cold, they arrived at Mauritius on 4th September, 1863, and heard with great anxiety of an insurrection in Madagascar, followed by the assassination of King Radàma II. and the accession of his widow Queen Ràsohèrina. Alarming reports were rife as to the political condition of the island and the dangers in which foreigners might find themselves. On account of these reports the advisability of immediately proceeding to Madagascar was very seriously discussed. Eventually, the Pearses and Mr. Kessler decided to leave for Madagascar by the first opportunity, while the others waited till reassured about the conditions of travel.

While at Mauritius they were much interested in what they saw of tropical life, and they write of such diverse topics as the beautiful vegetation, the varied attractions of the bazaars, the high rents for houses, the exorbitant prices for materials and the abundance of vermin ! One entry in the diary states, " On Thursday, I preached for the first time in my life to a coloured congregation. It was an anniversary service in the chapel of the Rev. J. LeBrun."

On the 19th September, Mr. Pearse writes, " Having made my final arrangements, went on board the *Jessie Byrne*, about three o'clock. Captain Cruickshank of the *Isabella Blyth* very kindly came and took us on board in his boat. As we passed the *Isabella Blyth* some of the hands on board gave us a hearty greeting." Of the ship itself he says, " The vessel is about 500 tons burthen, and is what is commonly called a ' bullocker,' *i.e.*, one used to convey bullocks from Madagascar to Mauritius, and is fitted up more for the accommodation of bullocks than for human beings. There is, however, accommodation of a sort for eight passengers or even sixteen, if two occupy one cabin. Our cabin is about two-thirds the size of that in which we came out from England, and opens, as did that, into what I suppose I must call the saloon, a small, nasty, dirty, miserable place, where we are obliged to take our meals but from which we always make our exit as quickly as possible."

The party arrived at Tamatàve, on 24th September, and received a cordial welcome from Dr. Davidson, who had journeyed down from the capital to meet them and render all the assistance that lay in his power. A few days were spent in making preparations for the journey and arranging their packages in convenient sizes for transport, these were carried by two, four or eight men, according to weight. They sent off 150 men, hired at the rate of three dollars (twelve shillings) each. They were entertained at luncheon by the native Governor and, while recording that " the dishes were all cooked very well," remarked that " the company, about twenty in number, were all dressed in European attire, but the great diversity of dress gave to the scene rather a ludicrous aspect."

On the Sunday, the opportunity of their presence was taken for holding an English service, and they were present also at a native service, where Mr. Pearse " married an old man of sixty to a young woman half his age."

The journey up country called forth from them the comments which are usual under such novel conditions ; they " wonder at the cheerfulness of their bearers, and the speed at which they go," they remark the bareness and airiness of the native houses, likewise the vermin with which they abound.

" The houses," as Mr. Pearse says, " are more properly

speaking, huts, many of them inferior to cattle-sheds, built now and then of wood, but commonly of stakes and rushes, or the broad leaves of banana or travellers' tree. The floor is the primitive earth or else is raised above the ground, and in that case is formed of laths ; it is always covered by a native mat.

"Instead of a fire-place the Malagasy mark off a place for cooking, stones answer the purpose of a trivet, and on these their cooking vessels are placed, grass or wood being used for fuel. There is no chimney and so soot is always left flourishing luxuriantly on the low roof and sides of the hut. There is but one apartment, and in this the native family do everything. The fowls, sheep, calves and dogs are frequently kept there too.

"Fleas increase and multiply and flourish exceedingly. There are other inmates too, even rats. Few cats or good dogs are kept, food for the rats is abundant and in many places they seem to swarm. You pass a night in one of these huts and you have them running steeple-chases about you all night, and moreover, they appropriate your property and hide it in their holes and they bite any clothes that are not put in a safe place. Mosquitoes also abound in some places, and lizards, scorpions and centipedes.

"These native huts are the only accommodation you can get ; when you arrive, your men rush as a matter of course into any hut they like ; the owners are hospitable and as a rule respectful to Europeans and will nearly always vacate it for your accommodation, being satisfied with a very small sum of money for their inconvenience."

They were much impressed with the diversified scenery; "sometimes," Mr. Pearse writes, " we were in a dense wood, and our pathway was entirely overhung with palms, again we were by the banks of beautiful lakes, and, now and then, when we were at a little higher elevation, we could see the fresh-water lakes on our right, and the mighty ocean on our left. Later on we crossed hill after hill, through beautiful valleys and through many streams. We also saw on our way the graceful bamboo and the tree-fern. Soon after reaching Rànomafàna (hot water), I, in company with Dr. Davidson, paid a visit to the hot springs, which are very rightly named, for the water is so hot, that I could not hold my foot over the place." Again, "our way lay through the forest and of the fearful character of the roads you can have no conception. Now, by roads full of deep ruts made by the rushing of water in the rainy season, we ascend hills of great steepness and now again we have to descend them, never travelling for five minutes together upon level ground. Deep ravines were often at our side, over which had our men but slipped we must have fallen." Finally they record their arrival at " Ambàtomànga, the last station on our way. The scenery was much like that of the South Downs. This was by far the largest town since leaving Tamatàve, and the house in which we passed the night much superior to any that we had before seen. Soon after our arrival Messrs. Cousins, Duffus and Parrett came from the capital (fifteen miles distant) to congratulate and welcome us. The meeting was very gratifying to both parties. We all slept, or rather passed the night, in one room, for many of us were so excited at being so near our destination that sleep was driven from our eyes."

On Wednesday, October 7th, Mr. Pearse records: " To-day we finished our wanderings and entered Antanànarìvo, the place where we hope to live and labour for Christ. We left Ambàtomànga at seven o'clock, our men and ourselves being in very good spirits. The Capital being situated upon high ground was soon visible to us, but it was not until between eleven and twelve that we reached it. A little distance from the town we were met and welcomed by a number of natives, also by Mr. Ellis and Mr. Stagg, the schoolmaster connected with the mission. Our entrance made quite a sensation among the people and our procession was of considerable length. We were set down at Dr. Davidson's house, where all the missionary brethren were assembled, and soon did justice to a good meal that they had prepared for us with great kindness. After dinner we went to see our house and then to tea with Mr. Stagg, returning about eight o'clock to pass our first night in our foreign home."

Mr. Pearse's early observations on his surroundings in Antanànarivo are given in a letter to his mother, dated November 6th, from which we quote : " The house itself is situated within a courtyard, surrounded by a mud wall. In appearance it is as much like an English barn as anything I can think of, only it is not so lofty and without the large doors. It consists of a building of wood, with a rush thatch and in size is eighteen feet by eleven-and-a-half. Glass windows are a luxury unknown to us ; light is let in at holes cut in the walls, to which wooden shutters are fixed, which we close at night. There is one apartment below, and another above ; the former we have made into two by a rush matting partition, but these are, as you may well imagine, very, very small. One serves as our parlour, the other as a room to take meals in, while the one above serves as a sleeping apartment and a store room for rice. Cooking (of which more anon) is done in a small detached building, and in that our servants sleep, eat, wash and do everything.   In the yard there are a tree or two, and a fowl house which I have built.

"The house has a very clean appearance inside, for it has been covered with new, clean, rush mats which the natives make very well.   At the back of the house, I have had a small room built, which is to answer the purpose of a study ; our house being so very small made this quite a necessity.   Of furniture we have wanted but little ; in our parlour is a table, two English chairs and two Malagasy ones lent by a native.   In the other room are a Malagasy table and a wardrobe. In the study there is simply a table.

" We have two male servants, the cook and another man, who is to fetch water and do everything else we want him to.   They have a dollar a month and their rice, besides any odd pieces of food that may go from our table.

"Our cooking, which is very limited in extent, the cook does to our satisfaction.   The fire is of wood and on the ground.   The principal vessel used is a large, three-legged iron pot purchased here ; in this the man bakes fowls and geese, as well as puddings or cakes.   Rice they cook in earthen vessels which can be bought here for a penny each.

" Coffee is grown and can be procured here ; tea we shall always be obliged to get from England.   Of rice, which grows in abundance, there are three kinds to be bought —white, red, and rice in the husk.   The former we eat, but we have not yet had to buy any, as we have had a large quantity given us.   Red rice, which the natives eat, is to be bought for about eighteenpence per bushel and they will eat about half that quantity in a week. Eggs are very abundant, and both hens' and duck eggs may be bought for twopence or twopence halfpenny per dozen.   We have had a great many fowls and six geese

given us ; fowls vary in price from twopence to sixpence
or sevenpence, according to the size and condition :
milk is good but scarce ; we usually get some every
day ; a quart bottle costs us twopence.

" In the town there are no shops or stores, everything
has to be bought in the markets, of which there are some
open every day ; a very large one is held on Fridays on
a space of open ground, at the foot of the hill on the north
west of the town, not far from us.   In it is sold everything that the country produces, meat, poultry, iron and
earthenware, eggs, rice, wood for building, clothes,
fruit, etc., with slaves in addition.   Fruit is not very
abundant at present ; we have had pineapples, which
cost about a halfpenny each, bananas and mulberries ;
other fruit, as peaches, mangoes, guavas, oranges and
lemons grow, but are not yet in season.   Native vege-
tables, of which there are a few, we have not yet tried ;
the potato flourishes well and can be bought cheaply.
I have planted some seeds from England and have
vegetable marrows, cucumbers, lettuce, turnips, onions
and radishes already above ground.

" Of dress, the natives wear but little ; the principal
garment is the *lamba*, which both the men and the women
wear ; an additional cloth round the loins for the men,
and an under garment for the women, usually completes
their attire.   The men nearly always wear hats but the
women never have any covering for their heads.   Many
of the children run about quite devoid of clothing.
The *lamba*, which is very becoming, consists sometimes of
imported calico ; but often they are made by the natives
of cotton or silk or the fibre from the rofia palm with
silk stripes, and some, which the slaves generally wear,
consist of very coarse native rofia cloth.   Many of the
natives, however, especially the men, seem to greatly

emulate European attire, and, somehow or other, have managed to get hold of a most miscellaneous collection, in which they look most absurd. If a party of them pass by, it is no uncommon thing to see them wearing trousers of all colours, green, pink, scarlet, buff, orange and blue, while their coats and hats possess the same diversity of colour and, if possible, a still more remarkable diversity of shape ! The dress of the officers in the army, on grand occasions, is equally absurd. They have got hold of old naval and military garments from different countries, and seem to vie with each other in making the most striking appearance. There is something like an organized army here, their weapons are old flint-lock muskets and native swords. In different parts of the town there are some twenty old English cannon, presented by King George IV.

" This city is situated on a very high hill ; the soil is red clay and full of rock. The roads are very bad, in fact they are so uneven and so full of immense stones, that it is with difficulty one can walk at all, and, after dark, it is positively dangerous to be about, for fear of falling. When the rain comes, it rushes down the so-called streets in torrents, causing deep ruts, loosening the stones and thus making the road far worse than before. There are, of course no vehicles about, since it would be impossible to so much as trundle a wheelbarrow. If we want to go further than we can manage to walk, we have to hire bearers who take us in palanquins. The natives carry their goods about either upon the head or shoulder.

" The houses occupied by the natives are very similar to ours, some having mud instead of wooden sides. The palace, situated quite on the summit of the hill, and above every other house, is a fine building of wood, with a roof of wooden tiles. The Tuesday after our

arrival we went there and had an interview with Her
Majesty the Queen. She received us very graciously
and expressed her pleasure at our safe arrival. The
day following, she sent us a present, consisting of one
sheep, twelve fowls and six geese, all alive, a large
basket of eggs and three of white rice

"Although an open supporter of idolatry, the Queen
is friendly towards us, and there is no impediment put
in the way of our prosecuting our work. The natives
are undoubtedly our friends, and are willing to receive
all the instruction we can give them, and they listen to
the teaching of the Word of God with attention and joy.
They are at liberty to follow what religion they please.

"The money current here is the French or Spanish
dollar. They also cut up these coins into small pieces,
so that when smaller sums are required, they have to
weigh the amount in small scales, according to standard
weights. This seemed very strange to us at first, but
we are now getting used to it.

"Our luggage reached us in capital condition the
Monday after our arrival. Nothing is spoilt, and of
the crockery, not more than about half-a-dozen articles
were broken. We have brought pretty much the right
things and at present want for little but groceries and
biscuits, for which we have sent by this mail. We
miss our English bread and butter very much !

"Flour cannot be bought here, and can only be procured by sending to Tamatàve, where it is very dear
and from which place a package of about forty pounds
will cost us twelve shillings for carriage. We drink
water, which has to be fetched from a considerable
distance in large earthen vessels.

"With the language we are getting on pretty well,
and by the aid of signs can usually make ourselves

understood. We have now settled down in this our abode, having made ourselves as comfortable as the size and condition of our house will allow. We are very happy and are under no apprehension of personal danger but as safe as though in our own native land."

As still bearing upon the habits and customs of the people, a few notes written by Mr. Pearse at a much later date may be appropriately introduced here.

" As there are neither gas nor street lamps, the natives seldom leave their houses after sunset, which at the latest is about seven o'clock. The light of the fires which they kindle for cooking their evening meal frequently suffices for the natives in their dwellings, or they use a rude iron candlestick, winding a piece of old rag round a lump of fat, which is placed in the receptacle and lighted.

" As there are no water works or pumps, the numerous springs which issue forth at the base of the hill are constantly surrounded by a crowd of slave girls, who convey the water in earthen jars, carrying it very dexterously on their heads, often ascending the steep hillsides without touching the vessel with either hand or spilling a single drop of the water. As our house was at the foot of the hill we sank a well and fixed a pump ; the terror of the natives in sinking the well was exceedingly great and it was only by going into the well myself and encouraging them that I could get them to continue digging, till we had reached a sufficient depth ; but when, after the pump was fixed, the handle moved up and down and a clear stream of water issued forth from its spout, they looked at one another in absolute amazement.

" There are no police in Antanànarìvo, but after ten o'clock at night, a body of guards parade the thoroughfares of the city proper shouting in a miserable tone through the hours of night, ' Who goes there ? '

" The staple food of the natives is rice, which is served twice a day about eleven and seven o'clock. The rice is thrown into water in an earthenware pot, and in about twenty-five minutes is cooked. It is served on plates, one usually doing for two or three persons, and eaten with native spoons made of wood or horn. Sometimes it is eaten by itself, frequently however meat, poultry, greens, broth, milk or honey are partaken of also. The Malagasy seldom cook the meat in joints, they cut it into small pieces, after removing the bones, and often cut the hide with the beef and so beef and hide, hair and all are consigned to the pot ! In the absence of knives and forks, the fingers are used. After the rice has been cooked and removed from the pot, the rice pot is again placed over the fire and the small quantity of rice, adhering to the sides of it, is baked till it becomes brown, then pouring in water, they boil it, and this liquid all classes are accustomed to drink after their meals. Other things partaken of by the natives are fish, dried and fresh, some kinds of beetles, hedgehogs and locusts.

" The natives take snuff to an enormous extent, their snuff being a mixture of powdered tobacco, wood ashes and salt. These are mixed and carried about in little snuff boxes, usually made of bamboo. Holding the vessel in the right hand, they tap it on to the palm of the left hand and this they dexterously jerk, not up the the nostrils, but into the mouth. After enjoying its pungent properties, they deposit it, under the edge of the rush mat or on the walls, in fact anywhere. Their houses are made disgusting with this stuff ; they take it wherever they are, even in chapel, and they used to make the side walls and the corners and mats so dirty that we had publicly to rebuke them, so that now many of them bring their spittoons with them !

" The cultivation of their rice occupies much of the time of the Malagasy, nearly every family having its own freehold plot of rice ground.

" Iron is very abundant and they make numerous articles in wrought iron ; the silversmiths make beautifully fine chains and exhibit considerable skill in copying any pattern with which they are furnished.

" Straw baskets of all sorts and sizes they make very well.   Many of the slaves hire themselves out as bearers of palanquins or luggage, and thus earn from fourpence to sixpence a day.   The freedom and liberty of British subjects stands in striking contrast to the bondage in which nearly every class of society is held here.   In the strict sense of the word, I question if there are ten free men in this place.   They are all in bondage to those above them, and this even up to the most wealthy and the highest in social position, for they in their turn are but so many slaves of the Queen.   All government service and all work for the Queen has to be done by the people freely, they get no money or return in any shape.   If the Queen wants a house, the people must build it and get nothing for their time and trouble. If she wants wood, the people must go to the forests, cut it and bring it.   In fact, whatever she wants the people must get it, and whatever work is required, they must do it.   Smith, tinsmith, silversmith in like manner must render their service.   No taxes in money are paid by the Malagasy and this personal service is demanded in its stead.   They are liable to be called upon at any time, and for an indefinite length of time, and when called upon are expected to leave all personal and domestic affairs and render what is demanded of them.

" By most Malagasy families considerable time is spent in the preparation of their graves, much more both in time and money being spent on their last resting-places than on their homes. A Malagasy will live in a poor, mean structure of clay or rushes, yet his tomb must be made of solid stone ; he will wear a dress of coarse material but his body must be wrapped in an expensive lamba. As soon as a man marries and becomes the head of a household, he sets about preparing the family vault ; property to a large amount is often spent in materials and labour and the construction will employ his leisure time and attention for years. The vault is often built in the courtyard within sight or within a few yards of the dwelling. Immense slabs of granite are employed for door, roof, shelves, and lining, and without any mechanical appliances these are dragged by crowds of men and women from the quarry to the place where the tomb is to be made. An indefinite belief in the existence of the spirit and its need of some of the articles to which the living had been used, led the Malagasy to bury various things in the vaults with their dead."

CHAPTER III

Beginnings of Work

1863 to 1868

THERE is no lack of books dealing with the earlier history of Christian missions in Madagascar. It will, therefore, not be necessary here to do more than compress the salient features of that history into a very few sentences.

The great persecution, marked by three special periods, *viz.*, 1837, 1849 and 1857, had come to an end with the death of the Queen Rànavàlona I., in 1861. The Malagasy Church, small though it still was, emerged from its ordeal with an increase both in numbers and vigour. The King, Radàma II., on his accession, gave full permission to the native Christians to worship in their own way, and set free those who were in captivity. In consequence there returned to the capital a large number, worn with disease, many of whom had for long been regarded as dead, but who were then joyfully acclaimed by their relatives and companions. The King also invited the return of missionaries to the island, to which call the L.M.S. responded by sending out, in 1862, the Rev. William Ellis, whose connection with Madagascar and interest therein had already extended over a large number of years, and following him, Messrs. W. E. Cousins, Duffus, Parrett, Stagg, Toy and Dr. Davidson.

These pioneers found three native Churches in the capital, with a total of about seven thousand Christians.

Among these, as a nucleus, they started work, with full
liberty accorded them to educate both children and
adults, to preach, form churches, heal the sick and carry
on all the agencies they might desire, for the spreading
of Christianity. They naturally very soon demanded
reinforcements from home and the party who left in
1863, and amongst whom were Mr. and Mrs. Pearse,
was sent out in response to this demand. Mr. James
Cameron, one of the artizan missionaries, who had been
ejected in 1836, also returned to the scene of his former
labours.

Antànanarìvo was at that time a collection of
villages on a long hill about a mile and a half in
length, and containing a population estimated at about
40,000. At the summit of the hill, standing about five
hundred feet above the plain, was the palace, a large
wooden building, afterwards encased in stone. To the
south, at the extreme limit of the hill was Ambòhipòtsy,
the village where the first martyr had been speared,
and where the second of the four Martyr Memorial
Churches was afterwards erected. Beyond the palace,
to the north, the ridge divided into two, one continuing
the ridge and terminating at Fàravôhitra, where the
Children's Memorial Church was to be built, over the
spot where Christians had been burnt, the other branch-
ing towards the west and sloping gently away to the
ricefields. Along this line was built the first Memorial
Church, that of Ambàtonakànga, not on the site of a
martyrdom but on that of the first native Church and
martyr's prison. Quite close to the palace, on the edge
of the rocks, over which the Christians had been hurled,
was erected the fourth Memorial Church at Ambônin-
Ampàmarìnana. Between the ridge going to Faravaòhitra
and that passing by Ambàtonakànga was the plain of

Anàlakêly, on which the weekly market was held and on which were erected the Church which came under Mr. Pearse's care, and the hospital. The spaces between these scattered villages have now been filled in with a more or less continuous line of houses, connected by good roads and differing entirely in architectural style from the houses of that early date, for whereas *then* they were almost all built of rushes or wood, with a high-pitched roof and that characteristic addition of long poles like horns at each gable, *now* they are almost all built of bricks, and roofed with red tiles, both wood and thatch having been relegated to the uncivilized abodes in the country.

Important political events had taken place during 1863 on account of the gradual loosening of the reins of government in the hands of the King, who proved himself too facile and pleasure-loving in character and too lacking in seriousness ; so that finally the more able members of his government revolted, seized the palace, gained command of the army and assassinated the King. With very little loss of life, the sovereignty was changed and the widow of the late King, Ràsohèrina by name, became Queen. It was this revolution that caused the uncertainty to the missionary party on landing at Mauritius, as mentioned in the last chapter.

The arrival of Mr. and Mrs. Pearse at Antànanarìvo was on 7th October, 1863. The first duty of the young missionary was the learning of the language, and his diary gives seven hours a day as the ideal of study to be aimed at. There were not at that time the valuable guides to that study which have since been prepared by the missionaries, but it was possible, by perusal of the existing imperfect grammar and dictionary, to obtain some insight into it ; and so, by this means, aided by conversation and scripture reading with some of the more intelligent natives, especially with those who had already learnt to speak a little English, gradual progress was made. Though the language itself is easy to learn, one is confronted at the outset by the difficulty due to every word being entirely new and unfamiliar to the beginner, having none of those similarities of form that the common origin of many of our European languages familiarizes us with.

Malagasy, being an oriental tongue, abounds in flowery modes of speech and proverbs, which greatly tax the memory, but which, skilfully used, make all the difference between a polished speaker and one with merely a working knowledge of the language.

By slow degrees Mr. Pearse gained such a command of this new tongue that he was able in a peculiarly direct manner to command attention and sympathy for his message, whether spoken or written. There is an entry in his diary for Sunday, 27th December, 1863, which becomes interesting in the light of his later skill. "Attended Anàlakêly morning and afternoon. Gave out a hymn and read a portion of the Word of God at each service. This is the commencement of what I hope will be many years of service for Christ in this country."

In March, he writes : " I have been able to make considerable progress in the language, so that now I can read very fairly and carry on a conversation without very much difficulty. I read and pray and now conduct my Church meetings." Early in April, he records the giving of a short address to those whom he had baptized, this was apparently the first public address he gave.

Early in the new year, 1864, Mr. Pearse writes to the Directors : " The Church at Anàlakèly being without a European Superintendent, at the request of the members of that Church I have consented, as far as I am able, to occupy that place for a time. It may lead to my remaining permanently in that position. The building in which we worship will hold about a thousand people and is usually quite full."

On the 5th of February there occurred the death from fever of Mr. Stagg, the teacher, the first break in the little missionary circle. Mr. Pearse was invited to succeed him in the oversight of the School and at once took in hand his new duties ; the number of the scholars remained at about 110.

From the month of December there had been over-shadowing the young missionaries a very great and unexpected trial. After less than three months' residence in the capital, there is this ominous entry in the diary : " Saw the doctor and received from him a sad account of my dear wife. He recommends returning to England at the first opportunity. May we be enabled to say ' Thy will be done.' " Tubercular disease had manifested itself in the lungs and it was only the impossibility of taking an invalid down country during the rainy season that prevented an immediate return to England.

Writing in March, he says : " I left England with my beloved partner in good health, having with me a strong desire to labour in this part of the Lord's vineyard. With this and with intellectual qualifications that seemed to fit her eminently for her labours, my wife promised not only to be a blessing to myself but to the Society. That the climate has had not a little to do with developing the disease, I think admits of no doubt, as from her infancy she has enjoyed unusually good health. During our journey up country we were necessarily considerably exposed, while since our arrival we have been living in a dwelling, which was, until recently, entirely without glass windows, and even now we have but one. The heavy rains during the past four months have saturated the walls, so that the mats in the room where we have been sleeping have been covered with mildew. We have done the best we could for ourselves and our friends have done their best for us.

" The Christians are very kind to us. Hardly a day passes but what some of them come to our dwelling, asking after her welfare and often bringing some little present. They frequently offer prayer with great earnestness."

On 22nd April there comes the entry: " Went to the market and bought a few things to take to England "; on the 30th : " paid a farewell visit to the Prime Minister in the morning. He expressed his regret at my leaving and hoped I should return. He made us a present of a native lamba. Wife very ill." And the next day, Sunday : " My last in all probability in Antanànarìvo." Mrs. Pearse's illness had become so alarming that with the advent of drier weather, the return to England was imperative. Her condition was probably all the more aggravated by her having to be hastily removed during the night, on account of a fire having broken out in a house near by. The houses, being all built of wood, almost invariably perished if a conflagration broke out. This time only six houses were destroyed and their own house escaped damage ; a few weeks later there was a great fire that destroyed no less than fifty.

The journey down country proved very interesting to the travellers, and there are many entries in the diary recording one thing after another that attracted their attention. It is pathetically evident that he was very far from realizing the gravity of the illness, but, in fact, the symptoms do not seem to have become more serious or alarming during the journey. A few days after their arrival at Tamatàve, however, Mrs. Pearse became suddenly unconscious, while on her way out to dine at a friend's house. There was no return of consciousness, and, after a night of anxious watching, her husband was thus suddenly called upon, at less than twelve hours' notice, to sustain the greatest personal loss that can fall to the lot of man. A sister of mercy rendered much help during that terrible night, help which was gratefully acknowledged and tenderly remembered. It was early on the morning of 18th May, 1864, that Mrs. Pearse died. The day before, she had risen as usual, and was able to read at their hour for prayer, the thirty-second Psalm being the passage chosen; during the day she expressed pleasure at some of the objects from the seashore that were brought to her. After a few days of great mental agony at Tamatàve, Mr. Pearse returned alone to Antànanarìvo, to take up again the work he thought had perhaps been renounced for ever. As he says : " The one has been taken and the other left. For what ? Surely that with increased love, with increased zeal, I should carry on the Saviour's work, doing with my might the work my hands find to do."

His letters show that his sensitive spirit was well nigh crushed by this blow but they manifest also a deep sense of the all-sufficiency of the divine presence supporting him during this terrible trial. Fever laid hold upon him after his return and prevented that absorption in the varied interests of his daily work, in which lay his chief hope of mitigating the poignancy of his grief. A scheme of some magnitude was awaiting his consideration, in the

erection of a suitable church for his congregation. Of
this, he writes: " The building in which my congregation
at present worship is of the most wretched description.
It would only be thought fit for a cowhouse in England.
My people, I am happy to say, have decided to make
an effort for a new building. They have agreed to
provide, dress and lay a course of stone for the foundation, to build the mud walls, to find the bamboos for
the roof and to procure and put on the thatch." He
himself promised to put in the glass windows, and sent
home an order for the glass to his friend Mr. Card, the
first of a very large number of such orders, that being
the particular form which his own personal contribution
to the churches erected in his districts generally took.
Later on the scheme was improved upon by the substitu-
tion of brick walls for mud, the use of sun-dried bricks
having been introduced by Mr. Cameron. The building
of such a church was a very absorbing occupation,
requiring the exercise of an infinite amount of care and
patience in superintending every detail ; without that
the walls are sure to be out of the perpendicular and the
windows anything but the desired shape !

His first sermon in the Malagasy language was preached
on 31st July, about ten months after arrival in the
island ; it was delivered twice, morning and evening
at different churches. He says : " From step to step
I hope to advance, till a more lengthened residence
among the people shall enable me fully and freely and
with an unfettered tongue to declare to them the glorious
Gospel." As he had suffered frequently and severely
from the fever, he moved into a larger house near his
own church and was thereby spared the continual inrush
of reminiscences, naturally suggested by his former
dwelling. Later on in the year (26th November),

he wrote an interesting account of progress in his work :
" Since our Church meeting of 30th December, 1863,
fifty-three members have been received into fellowship.
On Saturdays I have a meeting for explaining to the
natives portions of Scripture they do not fully understand, and for supplicating God's blessing on our
Sunday services. We have week-day services in houses
belonging to members of the congregation ; one is held
every evening at dark, the other in another direction
every Thursday. Our object is to attract the heathen in
the particular localities.

" The villages to the north of the city have received
some little attention, and there are evident tokens that
the work of Christ is progressing among them. In one
of them I stayed the night in a house of sacred asso-
ciations, for the Christians used to assemble there
secretly for worship in the days of the persecution and
the doors and windows were double, to prevent the sound
issuing forth. One pleasing feature has been the
erection of two new Chapels during the year, erected
by the natives themselves, with but little assistance
from outside."

After another twelvemonth he was able to announce
the completion and opening of his Church. " During
the past year," he says, " seventy-two members have
been added, making a total of 318. The new building
was publicly opened on 23rd November (1865). The
day was one of great rejoicing to my people and their
joy was shared by numbers of Christians from other
Churches. Although the services were not to commence
till ten, as early as seven the building was crowded.
The total cost has been about £200, half of which has
been raised among the Malagasy. The building will
accommodate 1,200 comfortably (squatting on the

floor) and on the day of the opening it was a gratifying sight to see that number, and more, listening with attention and interest to the preaching of the Word of Life. Alas ! the country distant from the capital is still uncared for. Their cry for help is loud." Others spoke of the building as being " quite a credit to the industry and zeal both of Mr. Pearse and his people, as well as an ornament to the neighbourhood."

Mr. Pearse had by this time been united in marriage to Margaret, daughter of Mr. Alexander Ironside, of Bonnykelly, Aberdeenshire, the marriage taking place at the Consulate in Tamatàve on 1st November, 1865.

In the following letter, giving in detail the diary of a week's work, much light is thrown upon the spirit of Mr. Pearse's work, and upon his methods for attracting the natives to Christ.

" *Monday*, August 20th, 1866. Met the adult writing class in the chapel (we have no schoolroom) at 6.30 a.m., and taught writing for an hour and a half. Seventy-one were present. This class was among the first things that I established and many of both sexes, although advanced in age, have made satisfactory progress. 8 to 11 —In school ; eighty-one present. This time I often grudge, but I believe it is well spent, for our hope in Madagascar, as elsewhere, is mainly in the rising generation. 1 to 2.—Visited the Hospital. There are twenty patients in at present. I go and converse with the patients once a week, and find many favourable opportunities of sowing a seed. Here, at the north end I find a poor girl, ill with spinal complaint. Here is an old man from the Bêtsilèo, reduced to a skeleton, and apparently very ill and awfully ignorant. I prayed with him, asking that the true Light might shine upon

MR. PEARSE'S FIRST CHURCH: ANÀLAKÈLY.

him. 2.30 to 5.—House to house visitation, principally among the members and families of my Church. I believe this to be a great power for good, both directly and indirectly. Here is one house into which I enter ; the father was out, the mother and children were at home. I squat on the ground, for there are no chairs. I begin to ask about the children, seeing many about. Can they read ? Do they go to school ? Neither. I tell them of our school and urge the mother to send them, quoting ' A wise son maketh a glad father.' We shall see to-morrow whether they come.

" Here is another house, so dirty and small, only about 12 ft. by 8 ft., and used as bedroom, kitchen, workshop, indeed for everything. There are two women there. They can both read and write. I ask ' Have you a Bible ? ' ' No, but we have a Testament.' ' Why have you no Bible, since you have heard that there are plenty ? ' ' We have not sufficient money to buy one.' (Four shillings is the price). I proceed, ' Could you afford two shillings and would you like to have one for that ? ' They could afford that and would be delighted. I told them to come to my house and they should have one. Surely to put them in possession of the Bible was well worth a visit !

" I pass an open door and see, within, a man and a woman spinning cotton. I know they are not Christians but I may say a word. I approach the door, and offer the usual salutations. They ask me in, so I enter and squat on the ground opposite them. We commence conversation and I ask them to tell me about their way of praying, but they are like all Malagasy, backward to say anything about their idols, so I tell them of our way, and urge it upon their acceptance. They make no promises, but at the same time they offer no opposition. ' No actual results,' you may say. I reply, ' I have spoken God's truth and let us leave that with them.'

" One more house. The owner is a member at Anàlakèly, but there are two middle-aged women, strangers to me, with her. I remark ' I have never seen you at Church,' which elicits the reply that they are not Christians. I tell them in a few words of the true God and ask them to accompany the owner of the house to Church next Sunday. They reply, ' We are old, what have we to do with the praying ? ' I remind them that whatever their age, they cannot do without rice, the staff of life with the Malagasy, and that equally great is their need of Christ, without whom the soul must perish. But they have another excuse ready, ' Look at our clothes, so bad, so dirty.' I told them that that need not exclude them, and put into their hands a small piece of money, saying, ' Buy soap with that, wash your lambas and I shall look all round the Church for you on Sunday.'

" *Tuesday*, August 21st. —Writing and school, as yesterday ; sixty-seven and seventy-nine attendances respectively.

" 3.30 to 5.—Service at Ankàdifôtsy, a village on the outskirts. There is but one Christian that I know of, living actually in this village ; she is a widow and it is in her house that we hold this service. There were about fifty present while many stood at the doors and windows. I delivered a short address from the words, ' Not willing that any should perish.' Amongst those within the house to-day were two or three who for several weeks past have listened at the door, but have never before ventured inside. We have established a school in this village and things promise well.

" *Wednesday.*—Writing and school.

" 2 to 4.—Bible Class for young men.

" 4.30 to 5.30. Weekly service at the Church.

" *Thursday*, 11 to 5.—Went to Ilàfy and held Bible-class. Thirty-three present. This class is not always held in the same village, but at four which I visit in turns. On the road, I entered into conversation with three soldiers and asked them if there were any Christians at their village. No. Then I asked about their customs. One replied, ' The keeper of the idol tells us the desires of the idol, such as money, a red fowl, etc., and these things we present to him.' I observed, ' Your god then is like us, you say he likes red fowls, does he eat them ? ' This provoked a hearty laugh, and they made haste to correct me. ' No,' they said, ' the idol does not eat them, but those who keep him do.' In simple words I them of the Creator and that He alone is God.

" *Friday.*—Sent letters, Bibles and books to a small company of Christians on the west coast, a month's journey from this.

" 8 to 10.30.—School.

" Preparation for Sunday.

" *Saturday.*—Preparation.

" *Sunday*, 9.—Service at Anàlakèly ; baptized eleven adults and eighteen infants.

" In the afternoon preached at Ankàdibevàva and Ambòhitantèly. (Three different sermons !)."

Some of the chief characteristics of his work in Madagascar are brought into prominence in this diary of a week's engagements. His method was the individual one, he tried to influence the people one by one. The early morning class for adults was a work peculiarly his own, and he also laid much more prominence on house to house visitation than did some of his brethren.

It came natural to him to be hail-fellow-well-met with
the people, and his easy manner and simple pleasantries
readily led to conversation with many whom it might
have greatly puzzled others to know how to approach.
Other notable features of his work were the teaching
of the children and the holding of the Bible-classes,
in the conduct of which he excelled ; the dissemination
of the Scriptures was likewise a point on which he laid
much stress.   One pastor tells us that in his house-to-
house visitations he used to ask for a Bible and when
the people realized that he would want one, they were
the more ready to become purchasers.

Of this period, the Rev. C. Jukes has given some
interesting reminiscences : " My mind has been carried
back to 1866, when, a bachelor missionary, I arrived
in Antànanarìvo and lived for a few weeks in Mr. Pearse's
house in Anàlakèly, he and Mrs. Pearse being in the
hospital residence during the absence of Dr. and Mrs.
Davidson.   Morning and evening he came over to see
how I was getting on, and help me with the difficulties
of the language.   One morning he came with two small
bottles of carbonate of soda and tartaric acid in his
hands, and taking off his coat and rolling up his shirt
sleeves, and opening a bag of flour which I had brought
from Mauritius, he showed me how to make a loaf of
bread !   We have never had a more sympathetic, tactful
and practical missionary than Mr. Pearse was.

" On my first Sunday in the capital I went with
him to his Church, and was struck with astonishment
at the large and attentive congregation of men and
women which had gathered, nearly all the people sitting
on the floor, clothed in lambas of clean white calico,
while the characteristic native ' click ' of approval
and pleasure which occurred again and again during

the delivery of the sermon afforded me no little interest
and delight. My inward soul cried: ' Oh, to be a
preacher like Mr. Pearse.' "

We may be permitted to interpolate that this was
fulfilled, when Mr. Jukes himself became one of the
ablest preachers in Malagasy.

At the close of 1866 he was able to record sixty-eight
persons admitted to Church fellowship bringing the
number of members up to 400. He says : " One very
pleasing movement has been made by the members of
our Church during the past six months, which is a sign
that the natives are becoming increasingly alive to the
duty of sending out the Gospel. We occasionally send
preachers to a few of the villages to the north of the
city to preach on the Sunday, but there is one village
some fifteen miles distant, which is too far for anyone
to go to every week. The Church have appointed one
of their number to live there, to do the work of an
evangelist, and they are now paying twelve shillings
a month towards his support. From the accounts
this native has sent me the number of hearers is increasing and an effort has been made to secure them a
small Church.

" I have lately received two letters from places at a
considerable distance from here. One is from Ambàtondrazàka, some five days journey to the north. The
writer, after thanking me for a Bible and some small
books I had sent, says, ' Send us a teacher or a preacher
or someone to teach singing, or *come yourself.*' I
purpose visiting this place next dry season.

" Another is from the west coast. A member of our
church was sent there some months since as Commander. Soon after his arrival he wrote to me, saying,
' We have finished a chapel and formed a congregation.

We wish for Testaments, hymn books and lesson books, for those I brought with me are not sufficient. Please also write to your friends across the sea, for perhaps there is a missionary who would like to come and live here and teach the people.' "

Mr. Pearse was present about this time at a feast given by a native pastor to bid farewell to a certain redeemed slave, who was sent as a native evangelist to Ambàtondrazàka ; the interest of this lies in the fact of Mr. Pearse himself being eventually stationed at that place.

In 1867 he wrote to say : " From time to time we are cheered to see coming amongst us those who in the past were persecutors of the Christians. A few weeks since, I was visited by one such who came to tell me that he purposed to attend our services, and he offered to give us a piece of land in his native village on which to erect a place of worship. At Ambàtofôtsy, where some few years ago the nominal Christians numbered merely fifteen or twenty, there are now some two hundred regular attendants, and the neat little church, built two years ago, is quite filled, and in fact, the accommodation is insufficient. The one great want in most of our village stations is more constant superintendence on the part of the missionary, but, with the great amount of labour incident to work in this city, that is impossible. We often wonder if it would not be desirable to take one from our number here and send him to a more destitute district. Mrs. Pearse and I would willingly go to labour in some district where we feel our labours would be more truly needed."

Thus early in their missionary career was their attention turned towards the deeper needs of the outlying districts, and the seed, the presence of which is here indicated, germinated and came to fruition in future years of service. But for the present they were kept from any premature departure from the capital, as, in the providence of God, events were advancing, though in an unexpected manner, towards extraordinary developments, in which the powers of all the missionaries were to be taxed to the utmost and their labours achieve an overwhelming success.

The Queen, who during her short reign had shown herself very tolerant of Christianity, though she never embraced that faith herself, was suffering from declining health and after moving about from place to place in search of health, she came back to her capital only in time to die. Mr. Pearse was in the city at the time, and writes to Mr. Card, describing what took place. "Ràsohèrina the Queen is dead. She departed this life on the 1st of April, 1868. She is succeeded by a relative who reigns under the title of Rànavàlona, a name which strikes terror into the minds of not a few, inasmuch as the Queen who persecuted the Christians so fiercely bore the same name. We think there is little ground for their fears and that in name only will the present Queen resemble the former one. In this country there is a public mourning whenever a sovereign dies, and during its continuance no important business of any kind is attended to. There are some strange customs, too, connected with this, for instance, everyone, men, women, children, slaves, and masters must have their heads shaved. You may imagine how the people all looked, completely shorn of their locks. We could scarcely recognise even those we knew best ! Also they are not allowed to wear any clothing over the upper part of the body, except the lamba. The men and boys must not wear hats (the women never do). The people must not build houses of mud, or weave cotton or silk or even lie on their bedsteads at night, until the expiration of the mourning, which lasts about three months.

" Before the death of the late Queen, but in anticipation of that event, an attempt was made to change the succession to the throne. The attempt was, however, a most complete failure and the principal parties concerned were speedily apprehended, and have been put in chains and confined in prison. There was considerable disturbance during the time, but no loss of life nor damage to property. Things have now resumed their ordinary aspect."

One of the pastors has supplied a few incidents relating to this time. He says : " There was a couple in the country who separated and could not agree, and the pastor was at his wits' end to bring them together again. He finally consulted Mr. Pearse, and they decided to invite the couple up to see him. So they were brought by the pastor, welcomed and shown in, and after the usual salutations, Mr. Pearse left them while he saw about the preparation of something to eat. This was served up, and then they begun to talk and the pastor spoke of their unhappy differences. He made them feel how really grieved he was at their story, then he warned them to be very careful of any causes of quarrel, and finally got them to promise to try in the future more than they had done in the past, with the result that they have lived happily together ever since.

" An example of his kind consideration was seen at the time of the return of Queen Ràsohĕrina from her visit to the coast in 1868, just before her death. When the court was approaching the capital, he inquired the names of all connected with the Anàlakĕly congregation

who were following Her Majesty.   On getting these
names he procured mats and sent round to each household a new mat wherewith to welcome the returning
members.   That gave so much pleasure that it is
remembered and talked of to the present day.

" When the old church at Ankàdifòtsy was in building and bricks were contributed by the congregation,
he went round to test all the loads contributed, so as
to see if they were hard or soft.   This impressed one
man very much and he desired Mr. Pearse to stop, and
let others employ their time over that matter, which
they ought to be quite capable of attending to.   ' No,'
he said, ' if the bricks are soft, the church will fall and
then I should be responsible for the lives of the people,
and beside that, if they see my care in examining their
work, that will make *them* careful.' "

With the coming of family responsibilities it became
imperative to build a more satisfactory residence, and
about this time, Mr. Pearse was very busy with all the
details connected with that.   Procuring the site,
making the plans, gathering materials and finally
superintending the actual erection all involved much
extra labour.   But in it all they received much gratifying assistance ; the plans were prepared by Mr. Cameron
and there was much interest shown by the natives in
the building operations.   One of them, writing about
that, says : " All the people who knew Mr. Pearse
wanted to show their affection for him by bringing
mud bricks for the new house.   From the officers down-
wards they came pouring in their contributions, quoting
the Malagasy proverb, 'One person alone cannot build
a house.'   So many bricks came that at last people
had to be stopped bringing them.   To acknowledge
these gifts Mr. Pearse cooked huge quantities of manioc

root, which was served up with native sugar, for the consumption of the visitors." Mr. Sibree says : " It may be remarked that this convenient six-roomed house proved so suitable to Malagasy, as well as European requirements, that it was copied in hundreds, if not thousands, of other houses, subsequently built in and near the capital."

During these few years Mr. Pearse had been developing his own methods of work, and had acquired a firm grasp of all its branches, whether in church, school or district. He had found his way to the very heart of the people, and already gained their love and veneration, and not only so, he had inspired his native co-workers with some of his own ardent devotion, so that both in the consolidation of work near at hand and the spread of Christianity further afield, they were willing and able to take their share.

CHAPTER IV

Overwhelming Progress
1868 to 1875.

WITH the new reign it soon became evident that the attitude of the Court to Christianity was going to be, not one of mere toleration, but one of the heartiest sympathy and encouragement. Here is an account of the early months of the reign and of the changes they witnessed, written on 1st January, 1869: "Most wonderful changes have taken place in Madagascar during the short period of the year 1868. The numbers of those who attend our places of worship both in this city and in all the country districts have greatly increased and the gospel of Christ has made marvellous progress. The national idols have been cast down, the native government has declared itself in favour of Christianity and the people have been encouraged to embrace it. Old superstitious laws have been abrogated and an enlightened code printed at our Mission press, and circulated among the people.

"There are government works for the manufacture of gunpowder, soap, etc., close to our house and, as on other days, so on Sundays, the bell used to summon the men to their labour. But for the past six months, the workmen have no longer been seen entering the gates on the sabbath day. On Sundays there used to be a large market near the road to some of my village

churches, where some 20,000 people regularly
assembled to buy and sell. Now the market has been
changed from Sunday to Monday and so there is a great
influx of attendants at the various chapels. The
gospel has found its way into the palace ; where the
idols used to be kept and gross superstitions observed,
a religious service has been commenced within the
last few months and the Queen and royal household,
together with some of the chief members of the native
government, meet morning and evening every Lord's
Day.

' On Christmas day all the Christians went in a body
to pay their respects to the Queen. The large courtyard
of the palace was full to the very gates. When the
Queen appeared and the natives had made their usual
salutation, a short speech was delivered to which the
Queen gave a brief reply, assuring the people of her
confidence in them, and expressing her desire that God
would bless them. After a hymn, they united in giving
thanks to God for the great things He had done for
Madagascar and in seeking His blessing upon the land,
and all its people. As soon as the meeting broke up,
we were all introduced to Her Majesty, who shook hands
with us in a most cordial manner and thanked us heartily
or what we had done and were still trying to do for her
people."

And again, at the end of that month, he wrote : " The
Malagasy year has just terminated and with it the last
remnant of idolatry has been removed from this city.
' Manjàka-tsy-ròa ' was more a symbol of royalty than
an idol. On the last morning of the old year it was
banished by royal orders. The new year was introduced
by the usual meeting of the sovereign with her nobles,
within the palace, but this year, as never before,

Christian hymns were sung, and prayers offered by some of the native preachers. One pleasing feature in the policy of the present government is their strenuous effort to suppress the drinking of rum. A short time ago a ship with a cargo of rum arrived at the port of Tamatàve. The custom dues were taken as usual in kind but soon after the barrels—some ten in number—were in the hands of the Government officials, they were rolled to the edge of the sea, the staves broken, and the contents allowed to mingle with the salt water ! ''

With the acceptance of Christianity by the Queen, there came an enormous inrush on the part of the populace, seeking education for themselves and their children, seeking also to worship after the new fashion approved of royalty. Much of this rush was inspired merely by the desire of royal favour, but, whatever its origin, it brought to the missionaries new responsibilities and new opportunities in overwhelming abundance. The children flocked to the existing schools, and new schools had to be opened all over the country side. Where were the teachers to come from ? Some had undergone sufficient training and were suitable for such work, but often a raw youth, just a little more advanced than the rest, was set to teach the others. There was no other course possible, unless, indeed, the opportunity were to be let slip and the general enthusiasm thwarted. And the same thing took place with regard to the churches. They were crowded with worshippers. New churches had to be opened in great numbers. In 1868 there were about 150 churches under the care of the London Missionary Society, in 1869 there were 468. The number of missionaries remained about the same. Pastors had to be found by these churches, and often men were chosen, lacking in spirituality and in almost every element of suitability, save only possibly the ability to read and a certain power of leadership.

If ever there was strenuous work done by a body of missionaries it was in Madagascar in the early part of Rànavàlona II.'s reign.

Mr. Pearse reports the events of 1869 in the following words : " The year 1869 has been one of wonderful change and marvellous progress. Its opening was full of promise, warranting the highest expectations, but we have seen greater things than any of us ever ventured to hope for. When we think, at the close of the year, of the increased growth of our churches, of the great addition to the number of nominal Christians, of the destruction of the idols and the uprooting of idolatry in this part of the island, as well as of the decided position taken up by the Queen and her government in favour of Christianity, we can find no fitter words, in which to express our surprise, than those so often quoted : 'What hath God wrought ? '

" Towards the close of 1868 we found our accommodation at Anàlakèly insufficient and so we commenced to raise funds for the erection of a gallery. Keeping up the character for generosity the people have earned for themselves, we raised what we hoped would be a sufficient sum. Mr. Cameron helped us nobly, and superintended the work gratuitously. Additional accommodation is provided for about 300.

" Churches have increased around us, and we have had a considerable number of transfers from our own to these newly-formed churches, but notwithstanding this and the removal of a small number by death, our statistics show an actual increase on our roll of church members. The majority of these are undoubtedly increasing in intelligence, and I trust, also growing in

grace. Their actual progress in Christian liberality
stands out very prominently. Guided by our experience
of the difficulty of raising money among the people by
special effort, we passed a resolution that weekly
offerings should in future be adopted and that all
funds required for every purpose should be raised in
that manner, the sacramental collection for the poor to
be the only exception. Up to the present date the
result has been most satisfactory, as the following have
been the sums collected since the passing of the resolution : £9 10s. ; £8 12s. ; £5 18s. We have by means
of this fund been able to join in the united effort put
forth by all the churches to evangelize the country
round, and we are now wholly or partially supporting
eleven native evangelists, stationed in various parts of
our district.

" During the past four months we have had various
opportunities of stating in the highest quarters very
clearly and unreservedly that we have no wish to make
the Church of Madagascar dependent on European help,
but that we desire to make it strong in itself and eventually independent of foreign aid. Many of the natives
appreciate this position and are anxious to bring
about this end. But the point at which they can be
left to themselves is yet far distant and in the meantime they need to be helped to help themselves.

" The returns of our day school are about the same
as those for 1868 (150 scholars). We have endeavoured
to make the school as efficient as time and funds would
permit but it is simply impossible for the missionary,
with the existing state of things in Madagascar, to devote
much time to his schools, and so this is to me one of the
most unsatisfactory departments of my labour. Mrs.
Pearse has conducted a class of women in needlework

during part of the year, and continued to render valuable assistance among the girls in our school. Our Bible classes at Anàlakèly conducted by Mr. Cameron and myself have been well attended.

" Our country district has greatly increased in extent during 1869. In 1868 we had ten village stations, this year we have to report twenty-eight. These are all within two days' journey of Antànanarìvo and do not include the more distant places among the Antsihànaka. Most of these stations I have visited during the year ; at the nearer ones I have held Bible-classes every week. To many of the nearer stations we send supplies on Sunday.

"As we review the past we have cause for deep gratitude and the most sanguine hopes. Anxiety however, is mingled with these on account of conscious weakness and the seriousness and extent of the work occupying our time and attention."

By this time Mr. Pearse had been placed in charge of an additional district, that of Fàravôhitra, about which he says : " It is now only some months since a congregation first met at Fàravòhitra. A few earnest and devoted men among the native Christians felt that it was very desirable to attempt to form forthwith the nucleus of the church, which should meet in the another church in the capital, as soon as the building should be completed. They accordingly purchased a plot of ground close to the site granted by Radàma II. for the stone church, and they raised a sum of money with which they built a large room for permanent use as a schoolroom, but which could be used for religious services in the meantime. This building was opened with a special service on July 9th, 1868, when a sermon was preached by the Rev. W. E. Cousins. The

ANTANÀNARÍVO.—ROAD TO ANÀLAKÈLY.

congregation continued to meet in this room until early in 1869 when the accommodation was found to be so insufficient that we removed and met in the still unfinished stone church. There were neither roof, doors nor windows, but the people preferred that inconvenience to the overcrowding. The church consists of 174 members, of whom forty-two were received during the year. Our congregation on Sunday mornings averages 600, most of whom have only recently commenced to attend Christian worship, and but few can read or write. A day school for boys and girls has been carried on during the year, with an attendance of 100."

" From many of the newly-formed churches in far off villages we are constantly receiving very affecting appeals for teachers and native evangelists. During the past week, one has come from a place six weeks' journey to the north. The writer says, ' We have finished a chapel, and write to tell you. It is large enough to accommodate 300 people. We have a school for adults and children.' We long for you intensely, that someone may come amongst us, and visit the church of Jesus Christ.' Another letter, from a place two days' journey away, says, ' The people come to the chapel, but there is nobody to instruct them, so that we are in real distress.' "

Of his building operations, Mr. Pearse writes : " Our hands are full of building, for everywhere around new chapels are in course of erection. We have given aid to over a hundred ; some will not have any great architectural beauty to boast of but they will meet the requirements of the villagers." At one village the pastor was blind ; but he was able to quote the Scriptures very correctly.

It was in September 1869, that another great step in the establishment of Christianity in the island was taken.   The idols, which for more than a year, had been banished from the capital, were then publicly burnt.

No particulars of this event in Mr. Pearse's writing have been found, but its historical importance is such as to demand more than a passing allusion.   We are therefore grateful to be able to quote vivid accounts written by others.

The Rev. George Cousins writes in the *Chronicle :* " There was nothing glorious in a Malagasy idol, nothing to awe, nothing beautiful.   A few pieces of stick wrapped up in a red lamba and decorated with beads and chains, a piece of chalk in a bag, a wooden representation of an insect—such wretched trifles were the objects of the people's reverence and regard.   Still, they have exerted a wide-spreading and most pernicious influence over these intensely superstitious people ; and if the gospel has not had to wrestle with the priests of a hoary-headed and elaborate system of idolatry, it has had to struggle with gross ignorance and darkness, ' a darkness that might be felt.'   *Kèlimalâza* (little but famous) has always been reckoned the first in power and influence of all the idols in Madagascar ; and even in his destruction he was honoured with the distinction of leading the way.   He was burned first, and the rest followed, as a matter of course.   His keepers had great privileges ; they had under their own control the life and death of their tribe ; if *they* were detected stealing or worse, they could claim release at once.   They were treated as nobles and could carry a scarlet umbrella, which is the badge of honour, confined, with this one exception, to princes and princesses of the royal blood. When Rànavàlona II. came to the throne, the special

privileges which had been theirs were taken from them ;
they were expected to do their share of government
service and to serve in the army, and were informed
by the Queen that as they were only nominally ' nobles,'
they must cease to claim the distinction and sink into
ordinary Hovas again.

" On the 8th of this month these people were at the
palace urging the Queen to return to the service of her
ancestors' idol and also asserting their right to former
privileges. Thereupon, the decision was come to forthwith to burn the idols, as " unless they had been publicly
destroyed the Malagasy would never have believed that
the Queen had really given them up.' So officers were
immediately despatched to this town, and arrived there
even before those who had been petitioning the Queen
could reach their homes again. The idol and its
trappings were brought out, and the officer, highest in
position, speaking, in the name of the sovereign, said,
' Whose is this idol ? Is it yours, or is it mine ? ' The
keepers could not but reply that it was the sovereign's.
' Then,' said the officer, ' if this is mine, says Rànavàlo-
manjàka, I shall burn my idol, for my kingdom rests
upon God.' Without further ado they set fire to
Kèlimalàza and burnt him and his umbrella and all
his belongings.

" Next day a general slaughter (of the idols) commenced. All the royal idols were committed to the
flames, and officers were scattered all over Imerina
engaged in the work of destruction. The heads of the
people told the Queen that as she was burning her idols,
of course they should burn theirs. Basketsful of
rubbish have been destroyed ; but, although rubbish in
our eyes, many of the people believed that it would be
impossible to destroy some of their honoured 'Penates,'

and they trembled as they stood round the fire in which they were blazing away."

" The Saturday following," says Rev. R. Toy, " the pastors of the town church met, and came to the decision that as the idols had been taken away from the people and destroyed, they would do their best to supply an experienced preacher to each of the (idol) towns every Sunday, and to pay a teacher to reside there continually. A collection was made among the officers, which amounted in a short time to more than a hundred dollars. Four teachers have now been appointed, all experienced and tried Christians, and last Thursday evening a meeting for prayer was held. Mr. Pearse gave the address."

Mr. Cousins continues : " The congregations are greatly increased, and new places are springing up at a distance from the capital, and not within easy reach. We are constantly hearing of people meeting together, and no one to preach to them. Every month shows one more clearly how utterly inadequate for the increasing demands of our work is the present small staff of missionaries. I cannot say that my conscience troubles me, but my heart does grieve most deeply, when I realize my inability to do what falls to my share. The native agency is strong in number, but deficient in knowledge and fitness, to instruct people in God's Word."

To more than 150 villages were teachers sent, with as little delay as possible.

The missionaries, who were actually in presence of the great awakeneng that these years witnessed, harboured no delusions as regards the comparatively low spiritual attainments of their converts. They simply did their best to meet the enormous demands so suddenly made upon them. Mr. Pearse says of those with whom he

had been thrown into contact : " While among those
who have recently joined the ranks of the nominal
Christians there are many imperfections, yet the
majority of them are making unmistakable advancement
in that which is good and true, and not a few are marked
by the simplicity of their faith, the fervour of their
devotion, and the sincerity and earnestness of their
lives. We, who know the people through living among
them, are well acquainted with their imperfections.
We are not silent when the members of our congregations
and churches deserve rebuke, nor lax in our endeavours
to lead them to be sincere in their profession, as well as
consistent in *all* their actions.

" The intellectual progress of the people is also satisfactory ; the demand for lesson books continues to be
very large. When the mission was re-opened, now some
eight years ago, the number of those who could read
was very limited ; now, there are multitudes able to
read. We have just received a large number of books,
20,000 hymn books printed for us by the Religious
Tract Society, and a part of the 20,000 Testaments and
200,000 portions of the Bible, which we owe to the
magnificent liberality of the Bible Society. Nevertheless, we have asked for another 50,000 Testaments to be
sent as early as possible next year !

" The evangelists who are stationed in the more important villages round, are, as far as my observation
extends, labouring with earnestness, acceptance and
success. Some of them are simple-minded humble
Christian men, and their conscious insufficiency for their
work, leading them to child-like dependence upon God
is very interesting. Our monthly missionary prayer
meeting is held in the various chapels in rotation and
even the largest of these is usually crowded."

In July 1870, Mr. Pearse visited a few out of the numerous village stations connected with his districts. He says : " The rough notes which I made will give you some little idea of the state of things in villages where the idols have been very recently cast away, and where the people have only within the past twelve months embraced the new religion. In some of these villages there has never been any regular instruction given ; the villages, owing to their distance, are beyond the range of any direct influence from us, and on account of numerous other duties it is only *very* occasionally that the missionary can visit them. The eagerness of the people for instruction is most pleasing and hopeful, but it is sad in the extreme that we cannot give them the instruction they want. In many of the village stations the people find the work of building and fitting up the chapel almost more than their resources can meet, simple though its arrangements are. At one place a neat chapel has been built, capable of accommodating 300 hearers, and the people tell me it is generally full. Formerly only two persons could read ; now the number has risen to nineteen, besides many whose accomplishments are still restricted to words of two or three syllables.

" The farther I get from the capital the greater is the ignorance I meet with.

" There is one large village I went to, with a numerous population round. A congregation of at least 800 could be gathered in a short time, were an earnest evangelist placed among the people. Alas ! the state of our funds renders it quite vain to hope for that at present. There is no one in the place who can read or write. If any written despatch arrives from the native authorities at the capital, it has to be taken to a distant village to be deciphered. Many of the inhabitants have never seen a European before, and there is not a little consternation and fear among them as we are seen approaching. In one place a woman who had become sufficiently bold to venture near in the morning told me that when she first saw me she fell down, and on the previous evening she had hidden herself. Another observed to my bearers that she had no desire even to look at me!

" At two places close together the people have put up a small rush place of meeting and in each there gathers a congregation of only about fifty. I asked the very natural question why they did not unite and form one congregation, but the reply was that the clan was different and so each must have its own place of meeting.

" At another village, with a very temporary building, I found the ordinary congregation is about one hundred, of whom but three can read. I was startled there, during the singing of a hymn, by two of the head men shouting in an angry tone to those who were doing their best to sing, commanding them to take care and do it well! While I was talking to the chief man of the village, of God and of Christ, our conversation was very unceremoniously interrupted by a woman wanting to know if I would not give her my white umbrella, or at any rate change it for her old blue one!

" My experiences however were not all of this character. At another place I was very much pleased. The evangelist, who has been stationed there for six months, has done much good. Already twenty-three can read and the majority of the inhabitants are learning. A neat chapel has been built, but it is already too small and there is talk of enlarging it. The singing, the behaviour of the people in chapel and their improved morals all testify to the good influence of the evangelist. When I was here a year ago, there was no chapel and only one young man could read.

" Another village that I visited is not more than half-a-day's journey from the forest. In this forest, the evangelist and his wife, who are now occupying this station, hid during the times of persecution. They remembered their trials and their prayers and requested that they might occupy the station. The change that has come over the place since my last visit is remarkable. Then, the women and children were all terrified and on my approach ran away in every direction, and even the men would not venture near. I got the most miserable accommodation, and it was with difficulty we could persuade the people to sell us food for an evening meal. This time, how different! Within a short distance of the entrance to the village, we could see a crowd of a hundred or more, headed by their chief man, gathered to welcome us. When they had led us within the village, one of the first things they did was to make us a liberal present of pork and rice for my bearers, while me they invited to partake of a meal they had already cooked. I found the evangelist and his wife deservedly respected and their labours appreciated. Now there is a congregation of about 400, and twenty-one can read the New Testament fluently. Upon their arrival they had met with much discouragement and were almost ready to give up in despair and return to Antànanarìvo. It was at that village that the people after consenting to a feast for the school children on Christmas day, drew back at the last moment, for fear that the teachers would make them *drink baptism* ! "

The Memorial church at Fàravòhitra, also at that time under the pastoral care of Mr. Pearse, was opened with special services on 15th September, 1870. The *Chronicle* says : " The Fàravòhitra church is built in a commanding position at the north end of the capital, and from the height and solidity of its walls, is a very striking object. On its site, in February, 1849, four Christian nobles, including a lady, were burnt alive, and the bodies of fourteen others, who had that day been thrown over the lofty precipice, were also consumed. In digging the foundations of the church, Mr. Cameron laid bare the charcoal and ashes which had remained from the fire ; and the first stone of the church was laid under the very spot where the stake had been planted."

Of the actual opening, Mr. Pearse writes : " The building was filled to overflowing at both services. In fact, in the morning, great numbers of people had to return to their homes, unable to gain admission. The people began to assemble as early as four o'clock a.m." Officers were sent by the Queen to represent her, and thank the missionaries ; special sermons were preached and the occasion was a very successful one. Mr. Pearse contrasts the present happy state of affairs with that prevailing twenty-one years previously : " Then, cruel and relentless persecution raged against the Christians ; their very name was hated, and they scarcely dared to meet together to unite in prayer and praise—not even in secret places and under cover of the darkness of night. Twenty-one years before, the sentence of death had been carried out and the bodies of eighteen Christians consumed in the flames which merciless persecution had kindled. To-day, eternal life has been offered to hundreds upon the very spot

from which the spirits of the martyrs had returned to
God, who gave them."

"I told the people that the money spent in building the
church had been collected by the young people in
England. They were astonished at this, and wondered
how the children managed to raise enough to build a
place which cost, what is to the Malagasy, a very large
sum of money indeed. I think the native Christians
are truly grateful to you and they have written you this
letter thanking you for what you have done for them.

"' Fàravòhitra,

"' October 24th, 1870,

"' To the Children in England.

"' We visit you by means of this letter. How are
you all ?   We thank those of you who paid money for
building the children's stone church at Fàravòhitra,
for we are exceedingly glad on account of your remembrance of us, so that you gave money to build the stone
house ; therefore we have a beautiful stone house in
which to pray to God. And the Fàravòhitra school
children also thank you and send their love to you.

"' Good-bye ! May God bless you !

"Says,

"' The Congregation at Fàravòhitra and
the Scholars.' "

At the end of 1870, the years since the resumption
of missionary work in Madagascar were reviewed and
Mr. Pearse contributes an account of his own particular
work, from which we quote the following : " The night
had been long and dark, when in the year 1862, the
Christian missionaries, sent by the London Missionary
Society once again landed at Tamatàve. But that year
was only as the dawn of day for the island. A few
faint streaks of light were visible. There was reason,

it is true, for *hope ;* but little ground, in the then existing state of things, both religiously and politically, for
solid confidence and joy. To-day, the close of 1870,
the gross darkness of superstition and heathenism have
been chased away—at least from this city and the more
immediate neighbourhood.

" In the number of church members at Anàlakèly
there has been a steady increase. During the seven
years a total of about 400 have been added to the church.
We are careful not to urge the people to take the
important step of becoming members, except as they are
led to do so by the teaching of the Spirit and prompted
by their love to Christ. None are received in any of
our churches under a shorter probation than four
months from the date of, application after baptism.
At a low estimate one half of our congregation can read
intelligently." He notes the rise of the number of village
stations from four to forty. " During the years 1863
and 1864 our church receipts were merely fractional ;
to-day I reported to our church meeting that the total
of receipts, from all sources, during 1870, was over £132.
The native Christians have, at least, *begun* to learn
to give and to think of others as well as of themselves."
" My receipts for books sold during the first two or
three years of my residence here were *nil ;* during 1870
the sum received by me in payment for such sales as
5,500 lesson books, 156 New Testaments, 1,200 hymn
books, 1,150 penny hymn books, 1910 *Good Words*,
was over £80."

A very important institution was founded in Antànanarìvo in 1868, *viz.*, the Congregational Union of Imerina,
which held its meetings half yearly. Mr. Pearse was
Secretary and gave a report of one of the meetings,
which is fairly typical of those gatherings, even up to the

present day. " The chapel (which provides accommodation for some 1,000 persons) was crowded to excess in every part, including the vestry behind the platform, while numbers, unable to get better accommodation, contented themselves by either standing upon the stairs leading to the gallery and clock tower, or by blocking up the various entrance doors. Representatives from over 200 churches must have been gathered within the building." Among other subjects discussed there were such topics as the Character of native preachers, Church discipline, Church and State, Behaviour in the House of God, and Marriage.

" The paper on Church and State was read by a high officer and was a word in season to many who have not yet learned to distinguish, at all clearly, between the business of the State and the work of the Church. It shows that the Government, as such, has no desire to rule the Church."

As time went on the many-sided character of the work for which the missionary was responsible became very marked, and in a letter, Mr. Pearse says : " It is a glorious, but a strange life, this missionary life ; you have to do so many things, and, following the example of the best missionary, become more or less ' all things to all men.' You have to see people on all sorts of business, temporal and spiritual, to write so many letters that a pile of notepaper vanishes in no time, to arrange this, that and the other, and to be, as far as possible, here, there and everywhere ! Each missionary wants six heads and a proportionate number of hands, feet, eyes and ears ! As, however, he has only one head and one body, you will infer that a considerable part of the work which lies in his way is necessarily left undone."

The ten years term of service was now rapidly drawing to a close.   After all the strenuous labours of those full years there was much need for rest and recuperation.   Hard work and many attacks of fever had left their mark on the strong constitution.   But still, a glance at the engagements for the first week of 1873, the year in which Mr. and Mrs. Pearse were to go home, does not suggest that there was much serious diminution of work ; there was a very creditable amount of work done as well as much preparation for it.   Sixteen chapters of the English Bible, one chapter of the New Testament in Greek, a chapter of Mr. Ellis' " Three Visits to Madagascar " and a magazine in the native language make a fair record of reading for one day !   There were two services on the Sunday, prayer meeting and two sub-committees on Monday, re-opening school and writing mail for Europe on Tuesday, writing annual report of the district and preparation of statistics on Wednesday, Committee meeting and proof reading on Thursday, and then a little later on service rendered to one of the brethren in time of illness, re-opening of training college for evangelists, and so on.   The report for the year 1872 is a remarkable record of progress.

" One of the things that it gives me much pleasure to record is the progress of education.   In 1869, the statistics of our schools gave a total of 556 for Anàlakèly church and the country schools as well.   The returns now show a total of 2,344.   In some schools where there were but twenty scholars, there are now ninety or a hundred.   In one village famous for its idolatrous superstitions there was no school until the early part of 1871.   At our last examination the number of scholars present from that village was 180, of whom eighty had New Testaments, a pretty conclusive evidence that they could read them more or less fluently.

" During the course of the year we have held com-petitive school examinations twice, among the great majority of the schools in the district. These we have found to produce a healthy stimulus among the scholars and to encourage the parents in sending their children to the schools, while the large gatherings occasioned by these examinations have attracted considerable attention to the question of education. At one examination, the Queen sent an officer of high rank to be present, who stayed through the day, and brought back word to Her Majesty of all that had been done. He took great interest in the proceedings and sought to encourage the scholars by giving small prizes in money to all who acquitted themselves most creditably.

" Systematic teaching of the adults in many of the villages has been carried on with satisfactory and promising results.

" At the close of 1872 we chose two native pastors for the mother church at Anàlakèly. One of them was formerly Lieutenant-Governor at Tamatàve. He was a scholar in the schools taught by the early missionaries and embraced Christianity long ago. For years he has been held in the highest esteem ; his family is quite a model one. The other pastor is a younger man who has attracted attention by his preaching powers for several years past, and has been in our Theological Institute. With the kind and judicious leading of his co-pastor, he will, I trust, fulfil all our hopes. One very pleasing feature was the decision of the church to do something towards the support of the younger pastor —a thing almost entirely new in Madagascar. They are

to give fourteen shillings per month, not a large amount,
but a step in the right direction.

" The preaching, teaching and visiting of former
years have been continued during 1872, though not,
I fear, with the vigour of the past.   A portion of what
little time has been left from public labours has been
devoted to writing for the press, and amongst other
things I have been publishing a few sermons, so as to
leave among the people, in an abiding form, some of the
simple lessons of divine truth presented to them from
time to time."

The statistics show very large and encouraging
figures ; in the mother church a membership of 607 and
attendance of 1,200 ; 160 scholars in the school, and a
total contributed during the year of £418.   There were
55 village stations and the figures, including them, bring
up the various totals to 5,340 members, 14,975 attenders,
2,344 scholars and £1,370 contributed.   The rapidity of
this growth is emphasized by a comparison with the
figures for 1868, only four years before, when there
were 765 church members in the whole district, 3,070
attenders, 332 scholars and £76 contributed, the number
of village stations being ten.

The importance of self-support as an aim to be kept
prominently before the congregations is evidenced by the
above report and by the following quotation :—

" No one believes more fully than myself that the
church of Madagascar should ultimately be made self-
supporting.   The Malagasy should support their
ministers, pay their teachers, buy their books and build
their churches without foreign aid, and they will do it.
But the pastors and others remind me in affecting
language of the present infancy of many of the churches
and of the ignorance of numbers in all the congregations

of their duty in reference to self-support." Alas, even in 1912, though great progress has been made, the same question of self-support is still very far from being solved! With the increase of the church and the increased area of operations, the difficulty dependent on the comparative poverty of the people is an ever-present one.

A month before leaving the island, Mr. Pearse paid a farewell visit to his district, and there were many evidences of the sorrow of the villagers at the prospect of the parting. He notes : " The people apparently very pleased to see me, and had food all ready cooked for me. The school children came to the house bringing a present of rice, potatoes and eggs and about a shilling in money. The schools from ten villages met together for examination and to say goodbye. At the close, parting speeches were made by the representatives of the various villages and small sums of money were given to me, accompanied by many a hearty desire that God would bless us and keep us and bring us back in His own good time.

" Held service and examination ; the evangelist and his wife both felt the parting and wept much.

" Gathered the church members and gave them counsel and advice. Had some interesting conversation with one young man, who told me some of his history during the dark days. He was the only Christian in his village and in every conceivable way the people used to annoy him, they would pelt his house with stones, refuse to give him fire if his happened to go out, etc. My last service before leaving ; several much affected."

" Among others we were privileged to say good-bye to was Rànavàlona II., the Queen of Madagascar. Hearing that we were leaving she sent for us and told us in a few words of her gratitude for what we had done for her

MR. PEARSE.

people and wished us ' God-speed.' She ordered her attendants to bring a couple of boxes of Reading biscuits for the children.

" Presents of various kinds were received by us, during the last few weeks of our residence, lambas, spoons, baskets, knives, money, fruit and poultry. A day or two before we left, a man arrived with a wooden vessel containing as much honey as he could carry ; it had been brought about twenty miles and was sent by some good people who thought that the children might like some on the way. Another day two lads came in carrying a basket slung on a pole upon their shoulders. It contained eggs, nearly two hundred in number, for our use during our journey. Thus in their simple unaffected way did the Malagasy give practical proof of their affection."

After these farewell visits to the district, there were farewell meetings in the church, and a feast was prepared by the people in honour of their missionary. To all this there was added the labour, far from light, of preparing for a fortnight's journey down country with a family of five young children, as well as for the voyage itself.

The actual departure took place on 21st May and Mr. Pearse describes it as follows :—

" On the top of a hill about two miles to the east of the city we found a company of about 3,000 persons gathered together. They were native Christians, met to take a last glance. Our bearers put us down and we alighted, while the people formed a circle round us. A native hymn was sung, after which the senior pastor prayed very earnestly that God would be pleased to take the missionary with his wife and children safely across the ocean, and grant, at no distant time, the joy of welcoming them again.   Then with tears and choked voices, they bade us farewell.   Strong men and women stood with the tears streaming down their cheeks, as in broken voices they said good-bye."

The journey down country was as difficult and trying as usual, and the rats rendered the nights horrible.   The voyage to Mauritius in the bullocker was long and very uncomfortable, and the lack of accommodation proved a positive danger to those, who were prone already to Malagasy fever and in no fit condition to " rough it."

A fortnight with kind friends in Mauritius to some extent ended the effects of these discomforts, and brought back a little more vigour with which to face the rest of the voyage.   Taking the French steamer *via* the Suez Canal, Mr. and Mrs. Pearse arrived in England again on 23rd July, 1873, and received a warm welcome from an unbroken family circle.

The story of the spread of Christianity in Madagascar was of such interest to the Churches that the " deputation " was in request everywhere to proclaim it ; Norwich, Cambridge, Brighton, Liverpool, Huddersfield, Doncaster, Coventry, Reigate, Lewes and Paisley, amongst other places, were visited.   Those were the days when a missionary's address was reported in full or even verbatim in the local paper and the wonderful work that had been accomplished produced a sensation wherever it was made known.

Not only so, but Mr. Pearse had other signs of good being done by his preaching in the home churches. One lady wrote : " I have long wished to make known to you, that, through God's blessing, I was awakened to a sense of my sins by the first sermon I heard you preach, about this time last year. The words ' He that cometh to me I will in no wise cast out ' struck me very much, and I had no rest until I went, and told Him my need of such a Friend and Guide, and now I feel filled with inexpressible joy and can say with my whole heart ' Bless the Lord, O my soul.' "

A brother-in-law, writing of him at that time, says, " His style of preaching is sweetly persuasive and earnest, his language very appropriate and smooth, so that every word falls into its right place and conveys the right meaning ; his action is moderate and graceful. His whole manner is so unaffected and gentle that he makes friends wherever he goes. When on deputation work in the north, the gentleman at whose house he had been staying exchanged his ticket for a first-class one ; and whilst talking with him at the carriage door two ladies got in, who after the train started asked if they understood he came from Madagascar ; and when they parted asked for his private address." From this there followed many acts of kindness and interest on the part of these ladies, who proved to be ladies of title.

The Rev. Robert Robinson, Home Secretary of the London Missionary Society wrote to him : " A young undergraduate of Cambridge has just told me that one of his fellows, a fine, highly-intellectual Christian young man, was so impressed by your missionary sermon at Cambridge that he has resolved ere long to offer himself for missionary service. Thus you see the good Lord permits some both to sow and to reap ; all are not thus favoured as you are."

As much time as possible was spent in medical study and dispensary practice, opportunities for which opened up in London. In this way he tried to fit himself for whatever work the future might bring and, when the question of return to Madagascar ripened, it was decided by the Directors to accede to his wish to go as a pioneer to some other field than the capital.

The province of Antsihànaka, which he had visited in 1868, was chosen as his sphere of labour. This decision was embodied in a resolution of the Directors: "That the Directors record with pleasure their high appreciation of the Christian character of Mr. and Mrs. Pearse and of their work in the Imèrina district, and of the self-denial and zeal which have prompted them to desire to devote their future efforts especially to the advancement of the Kingdom of Christ in the Antsihànaka country."

The brethren in Madagascar recorded their feelings in the following: "That this Committee deplores Mr. Pearse's removal from Antanànarìvo, where his loss will be deeply felt both by Europeans and natives, but believes that his well-earned reputation, his knowledge of the habits and language of the people, his intimate acquaintance with all the details of missionary work in Madagascar, and his kind and conciliatory disposition will be of very great service to him in his new sphere of labour."

CHAPTER V

Antsihànaka and the Native Beliefs

THE Antsihànaka Province, to which Mr. and Mrs. Pearse were sent in 1875, lies about a hundred miles to the north-north-east of Antanànarìvo. Before following them into their work and describing the agencies which they brought to bear on the benighted inhabitants of that region, it will be well to obtain some idea of the characteristics, both of the province itself and of its inhabitants.

The province occupies a deep depression between the two ranges of high forest-clad mountains that run up the east side of Madagascar for the greater part of its length. In shape it is roughly an oval, about a hundred miles long by twenty-five wide ; three-fifths of its surface consists of plain, and two-fifths of swamp and lake, the largest lake in the island, Lake Alaòtra, being in Antsihànaka.

The towns and villages are mostly found round the edge of the plain near the rising ground ; the plain itself is covered with grass which supports innumerable cattle, and the swamps abound in reeds and rushes which are largely used for domestic purposes. Wild fowl, fish and crocodiles all swarm in the waters. The province is extremely fertile and all produce grown there is especially well-developed. In the valleys between the mountain ranges and also in the swampy ground are vast ricefields. Near the villages much sugar-cane, of a large variety, is cultivated and from this the natives manufacture the rum which is their bane.

The population was estimated at about 40,000. The natives are known as the Sihànaka tribe, meaning " the people by the lake." They were subjugated by Radàma I., somewhere about 1820, and a garrison of Hova was sent down to live amongst them ; there has continued to be a large Hova population ever since. The natives, however, differ from the Hova in many respects, in appearance, dress, habits and language. They are somewhat darker in hue and less delicate in build than the Hova ; the hair, whether of the men or the women, is worn long and plaited into tassels, with a little knot at the end. The dress in those days was, for the men, a loin-cloth wound several times round the waist ; for the women, a long garment reaching to the ankles ; and, for both sexes, the *lamba* wrapped round the upper part of the body and flung over the shoulders. The dress of the women was frequently made of a dark material, so as not to betray dirt so easily, and though in course of time it became intolerably dirty and greasy, it was not washed, because the effect of washing is only to make it wear out all the sooner ! The Sihànaka, however, were as a people more fond of ornament than the Hova and indulged in chains, necklaces and armlets of silver, or of beads, which were worn on all festive occasions. The silver chains were sometimes strings of coins, chiefly the large five-franc pieces, pierced and strung together, and sometimes thick heavy links of native make, which were worn even eight or ten rows deep. Sometimes coins would be worn at the end of the tassels on the hair.

The houses were built of reeds and thatched with rushes ; the average size was about eighteen feet by

twelve. In houses near the lake a raft was often laid
on the floor, so that, should the waters rise and inundate
the dwelling, the raft and all that was on it simply
floated on the surface! The family possessions were
kept in baskets placed on shelves round the walls,
and sometimes the cooking pots were placed there too.
Of furniture there was none. There were also no
chimneys, so that soot accumulated everywhere,
especially on the cobwebs, which formed festoons in
generous profusion under the roof.

The occupations of the villagers were limited. To
the women were apportioned the household duties of
preparing, cooking and serving the rice, making mats,
baskets and earthenware pots and dishes ; the men
looked after the sowing and reaping, tending cattle and
building. Both sexes engaged in fishing, and the old
people in distilling rum.

The rum-drinking was universal. The spirit was
distilled in the village, and sold at the rate of about
twopence a quart. There was no sense of shame in
drinking it, men, women and children partaking freely,
and no event of family interest, no ceremony of any
kind could be considered properly honoured without
the consumption of enormous quantities of this vile
stuff. Hospitality was incomplete without it ; even the
visit of the missionary was celebrated in such fashion,
and one missionary tells of no less than thirty bottles
having been brought in his honour ! They could not
understand his declining the compliment ! An individual would consume as much as two quarts of un-
adulterated rum in an evening. The obvious results
were demoralization and degradation, appalling, complete and broadcast.

Mr. and Mrs. Pearse were stationed in the chief town

of the province, known as Ambàtondrazàka, or the town "at the stone of Razàka," at the time of their settlement consisting of some four hundred houses, erected at the end of a long hill. The houses were mostly of the style already described, but there were a few of a better type, mud-walled, in the occupation of the Hova. Three stockades of timber surrounded the Governor's house.

Mr. Pearse said, in describing the town : " The houses are erected without any regard to order or regularity—higgledy-piggledy, anyhow. There is but one main thoroughfare, which is at all seasons in a filthy condition ; refuse is cast into it, bullocks and pigs are slain, quartered and then sold there, and bones could be gathered up by basketsfull."

There was already in the town a church, capable of accommodating 500, erected on the site of a house wherein some of the native Christians had been imprisoned during the persecution.

So much for the Sihànaka, their surroundings and occupations. What, however, was the nature of their religious beliefs and practices ? Briefly, it is questionable whether they had any but the most meagre ideas on religious matters. The ancestral spirits, offended or neglected, were regarded as the most potent objects of dread. Offerings to appease and charms to propitiate these were the chief instruments of worship. Diviners were the authorities who gave instructions concerning the necessary practices. But all, diviners, offerings and spirits were very apt to be neglected during prosperity, and only remembered when sheer necessity prompted. There were no stated meetings for worship, neither was there any organized religious system ; the people were extremely reticent in speaking about their beliefs, and could give no why or wherefore for their practices, except that the diviner had thus enjoined. The root-idea impelling the Sihànaka, and, in fact, all the non-Christian Malagasy, is fear, fear of the power of the dead, and fear of the occult influences of the living, as shown by witchcraft and the evil eye. To avert these, the diviner must be consulted, and every event of importance and every scheme projected demanded his assistance. He would arrange his beans—usually a large acacia seed—and move and transpose them, muttering his incantations the while, and at the end declare the result, announcing the conditions of time and place necessary for the success of the project, the things to be avoided, the offerings required by the spirits and not forgetting the reward suitable for the diviner himself. If sickness or misfortune befall, a similar process is gone through to discover the reason ; witchcraft is usually suspected, and the antidote, it is the business of the diviner to find out. There are general prohibitions, the infraction of which is always to be dreaded ; these vary in different villages, and even in different families. Fowls must not be eaten for fear of the offender being attacked by the dancing mania, nor certain parts of the ox for fear of loss of property ; food must not be partaken of at the fireside of a stranger ; pork and certain herbs were never allowed at all. There were lucky and unlucky days, work must not be done on Tuesdays or Thursdays, some villages must not be entered on certain days ; children born on unlucky days must be done away with. The flight of certain birds across the path was always regarded as an adverse sign and the expedition was given up.

To keep the ancestral spirits in good temper, sacrifices were offered, oxen slain at the tomb and libations of rum and honey poured out, specially during illness or after recovery, after a birth or on returning from a successful expedition.　There was a recognized order of ritual to be carried out, but the procedure was of a very involved and intricate character.

During sickness, exorcisms were used ; the evil was represented by bits of wood, rag or earth ; someone especially chosen pronounced the exorcism and threw these things away to the southward, all the people shaking their robes and spitting towards the door to help the evil out !　The sick were constantly moved from house to house, for fear of the house being be-witched, and visitors were often forbidden, for fear of the evil eye.

Charms of various kinds were used very largely indeed, such as bits of sacred wood, bone and iron, crocodile's teeth, or small models representative of their desires ; a collection of these objects was worn ; some were mingled with ashes and castor oil, and kept in the tip of the horn of a certain kind of ox.　These things were provided by the diviner, blessed by him and often sold for an exorbitant amount in money or oxen.　Each had its special significance, such as giving success to an expedi-tion, averting danger from crocodiles or from drowning, or securing love or offspring.　The non-success of the wearer of the charm was always put down to the em-ployment of more potent witchcraft by others or to the infraction of some of the multitudinous injunctions laid down by the diviner.　It was never the fault of the diviner himself !

When sickness was advancing to a fatal termination, not infrequently the patient would announce that he had seen the spirits of certain relatives who were come to fetch him to go " there "—the destination not being particularized ! Death was regarded as a great evil to be averted by all possible means, but when it became inevitable it was accepted quite philosophically.

Among the burial customs there are many of an extraordinary character, of which some may be mentioned as illustrating the beliefs of the Sihànaka. In contrast to their squalor during life, at the funerals there is great ostentation, with a view to showing the importance and wealth of the deceased. This is probably because he has now joined the ancestors and must, like them, be treated in a complimentary manner ! A very great slaughter of oxen takes place, far beyond the needs of the household, even though it be enhanced by the arrival of relatives from far and near. The heads of the oxen are retained to grace the tomb ; the oxen themselves are supposed to accompany the deceased   it would not do, they say, to slaughter only one ox, as in that case all the time of the spirit would be taken up in chasing it !

In the case of the wealthy, the body was kept for a week, during which time there were orgies of drinking, singing and lamentation. The amount spent in one way and another during the funeral was enormous, as much as £60 being expended on winding-sheets and rum, and perhaps as many as a hundred oxen would be slaughtered. At the close of the ceremony, an old man came forward to curse the unknown individual who had bewitched the deceased and caused his death.

Near the tomb there was a special embellishment peculiar to the Sihànaka. A pole, with two branches resembling the horns of an ox, was erected, on which were hung such things as the drinking vessel, looking-glass and even bedstead of the deceased ; the heads of the oxen were impaled on posts set up near this. In the grave were buried small articles of particular value, such as his knife, comb, snuffbox and spear, also a bottle of rum. It is evident therefore that the spirits were supposed to enjoy, in the beyond, an existence similar to the mundane. There seems little of beauty or inspiration connected with the beliefs or practices of the Sihànaka. Ignorance, superstition and indifference characterized their religious observances. Against some of their practices it was necessary for the missionary to wage war, but there was no call for any particular measures such as might be demanded in the case of a highly organized heathenism. It was the simple and ordinary missionary work which he was going to employ to enlighten their ignorance, remove their fears and rouse them from indifference; and there was no better method for bringing them to a fuller religious development than the living of the Christian life in their midst.

CHAPTER VI

The Missionary's Own Story

MR. PEARSE has himself summarized his life and work in Antsihànaka, and we will let him tell his own tale.

" Having said good-bye to relatives and friends and five beloved children, accompanied by my wife and our little girl, I left England the second time for Madagascar. Four months after starting from London, we anchored off Fènoarîvo, a village on the east coast of Madagascar, north of Tamatàve ; there we disembarked, and there were landed our numerous packages— made all the more numerous by the fact that we were going to try and open a new mission among the Sihànaka. That we had escaped the perils of the sea, that we had voyaged in a small sailing barque some 10,000 miles without any serious mishap, and that we were once again safe and sound and well in the land of our adoption were blessings for which we were glad and grateful. Now, however, real difficulties centred round the fact that we were to take an unusual route into the interior, and consequently bearers for ourselves and our goods were not to be found.

" Imagine yourself recently landed at a small coast village, with your wife and ten months old child, and with a large quantity of luggage representing more or less all that you will want for yourself and family, and for your work for, say, five years to come ; furniture, the things necessary for domestic and personal use, medicines, Bibles, slates, pencils, copybooks and the doors and windows for the house you hoped to build. Imagine yourself some 200 miles away from your destination in the interior and without railway, cab, tramcar, waggon, cart or even wheelbarrow. We, however, had not to imagine it ; we had to face the stern reality !

" Fortunately I knew the language, and in our difficulties I had an inspiration. While living in Antanànarîvo I had once paid a short visit to the town for which we were bound, and while there I had made the friendship of the principal chief of the district, who, like all other natives in a similar position, had very great local influence and authority. To this chief I wrote. I told him that we had arrived, that our purpose was to come and live with him and his people, to preach the gospel to them and teach them, and to help them in every way we could, but that we found it impossible to get to them, and then I asked him to send to us without delay 200 men. The letter containing this modest request was despatched by two special couriers, who were to deliver it and bring back the answer. After about three weeks this came, and this is what the chief said, ' We have received your letter telling us that you have trouble in getting men to carry your luggage, and asking help from me. Behold, then, the 200 men you ask for, who will carry you and your goods to Ambàtondrazàka, on account of our joy that you are coming to live among us.' The letter was brought by three underchiefs and a few days later the 200 swarthy fellows arrived, bringing long stout bamboo poles and strong creepers and ropes with which to lash our goods thereto for conveyance up to the interior.

" The repacking of our goods occupied a few days, and then we started, eight men carrying Mrs. Pearse and the child in an open basket-like palanquin, another eight carrying myself, four carrying a big case here and two a small one there, some carrying doors for the house, some with crockery, pots and pans, bedstead and bedding, flour and sugar, and so finally the whole party was on the way.

" The journey was difficult and trying enough. The hills were steep, the tropical forests dense and almost impenetrable, the passes sometimes so narrow that we had to widen them to allow of our passing through. There were no hotels or comfortable homes of hospitable friends *en route*, so that we had to pass the nights in native huts. These were small and dirty, and infested with vermin and abounding with rats which enjoyed themselves running all about us from darkness till dawn !

" The morning of the twelfth day found us commencing the final stage of our journey. It was, I remember, a beautiful morning, a few light clouds were floating under a clear blue sky and volumes of white mist were rolling from the valleys towards the west, and in the brightness of that morning, I could hardly help seeing a promise of happy results to follow the work we hoped soon to commence. About ten o'clock we reached the summit of a high hill from which Ambàtondrazàka came into view and two or three miles ahead we could see a crowd of people waiting for our arrival. Another company was waiting an hour's ride away on the outskirts of the town. The heavy luggage had got there before us. A native band was on the scene, consisting of two drums, a cornet and two flutes, and this struck up a lively tune. After a brief halt we

formed a procession into the town ; the band led the
way, the heavy luggage followed, Mrs. Pearse and the
child came next ; I took the next position and the
natives who had come out to meet us formed the rear-
guard.

" The governor, to whom I owed the bearers, met us
in the middle of the town and welcomed us most
heartily.   At this moment there was an affecting scene.
Our old nurse from the capital was there to meet us,
and rushed forward, with demonstrations of delight,
and immediately took the baby into her charge.   The
governor then led us to a compound in which were three
newly-erected huts, which he placed at our disposal.
These huts formed our home for nearly two years ; the
first was about fourteen feet by twelve, and served
for kitchen, dining-room, drawing-room and library ;
the second, about twelve feet by nine, was store-room
and afterwards also dispensary, while the third, of like
dimensions, we made our bedroom.   Such was our
early home, but though of extreme simplicity we found
much happiness therein.   Our chief troubles were two :
in the rainy season we could not keep the wet out and
sometimes had to get under the table to secure sufficient shelter, and also in the rainy season the mosquitoes
appeared in myriads and drove one to distraction !

" In their simple native way the people showed their
pleasure at our arrival by bringing presents.   During
the course of the day, the governor came and in a short
speech said, that we must be tired and hungry after our
journey, so they had brought a little food to refresh us,
the little food consisting of several live fowls and geese,
about three-quarters of an ox, also baskets of rice, fruit,
eggs and sweet potatoes !   Another day two chiefs
came with their followers and presented a large pig,

four fowls and a huge basket of white rice. One man prettily expressed the pleasure our arrival had given by saying it was as if each house had suddenly become possessed of a thousand dollars. No European had before settled in that part of Madagascar and as no woman or child had ever appeared among them, we were objects of great curiosity in the eyes of the natives, and day after day they came round us in large numbers. They wanted to look at us and to see our things, the clock, the looking-glass, the pictures, the lamp, the bedstead, knives and crockery, but what pleased them more than anything else was a large dressed wax doll,— one of the kind made to open and shut its eyes. That they were never tired of looking at and we used to get rare fun with it. We would present it with its eyes closed, and say to the visitors, ' She is asleep now and you must try and wake her up,' whereupon they would clap their hands, and shout and shout again, but all to no purpose ! Then at the right moment the wire would be pulled unnoticed by them, and the doll would open its eyes, when the crowd would gaze wide-mouthed, in the greatest astonishment, and with signs of not a little fear, they would exclaim, 'It is without doubt a child, but without life. Life is the only thing you white people cannot give ! '

" On our arrival, we found the Sihànaka living in a state of primitive simplicity and universally ignorant and superstitious. They knew nothing of the love of God, nor of the salvation which there is in Jesus Christ. Very many had never even heard the Saviour's name. Not long after our arrival, an old woman was brought to me, quite blind in one eye and nearly so in the other, and I was not able to do anything for her. ' But,' I said, ' if you trust in God, and believe on Jesus and

follow Him, you will be all right when you get to the
better world, to which God will take you.' And then
I asked her, ' Do you know the Saviour's name ? '
With a smile at my asking such a question, the poor
old woman said, ' What do we poor Sihànaka know ? '

"We did not find any idols, in the strict sense of that
term, but we found gods many in the form of charms,
which exerted a great influence on their life and conduct.
Their belief in witchcraft was also universal, and to
account for sickness or even death, it was quite common
for us to be told, ' Oh, he has been bewitched ! '

"During the building of the mission house we had
personal experience of their use of charms, for one
morning we found that during the night a charm had
been thrust into the thatch of our house. It consisted
of an unfinished rush basket, containing an addled egg,
a dead frog and a tiny packet of earth, said to have
been taken from a grave. The first two things spoke
of non-success and the others suggested death ; it was
generally expected that our house would collapse, and
we ourselves die, but to their astonishment neither of
these calamities happened.

"Looked at as a whole, our work was of a most
varied kind. I was, verily, pretty much of a Jack-of-all-
trades ! I was in turn carpenter and joiner, bricklayer
and plasterer, architect and builder, plumber and glazier,
whitewasher and paper-hanger, author and bookseller,
physician and surgeon, likewise dentist, and constantly
teacher and preacher ! In all these ways we tried to
uplift those among whom we lived and to exert an
influence over them in favour of civilization, education
and Christianity.

"Preaching the Gospel was emphatically our work.
I strove to make the natives know Jesus Christ, and

sought to lead them to the Saviour, that they might learn from Him how to live and how to be happy both in life and death, because of a blessed hope through Him. They did not understand that this was our object ; in fact they did not know what it meant. The current idea at first was that we had come to trade, and many were the enquiries we had for calico, print, knives, plates, guns, gunpowder and other things. I soon undeceived them ; the first Sunday that I addressed them I tried to give the trumpet no uncertain sound. Taking as my text, the words ' Philip went down to Samaria and preached Christ to the people,' I told them that I had come to do the same for them.

" My sermons consisted of the ' milk ' of the word, suitable for a congregation of ' babes ' ; but the most elementary truths, expressed in the very simplest terms, often failed to be understood. After service one Sunday morning two women followed me to our house, asking to see the celebrated doll. I tried to draw them into conversation, and asked them what the preacher had said. 'Don't know,' said one of them. 'Who did he tell you the Saviour was ? ' ' Don't know,' again. ' Well, did he say that God is harsh and cruel and does not care for such poor, ignorant people ? ' ' Oh yes, that was just what he said,' was the reply. That was immediately after I had been preaching, as simply as I knew how, from ' If ye then, being evil, know how to give good gifts, etc.'

" I am not able to say much concerning the direct spiritual results of our labours among the Sihànaka. But few conversions were heard of during our six years of toil among them. We had the honour to be pioneers ; our work was to clear the ground, to gather out some of the hard stones of ignorance and superstition, to plough the fields and scatter broadcast the good seed. Others had more of the joy of reaping.

" Next to the preaching, the teaching of adults and children formed an important element in our work. Soon after we were settled, six o'clock in the morning found me with a class of adults around me, to whom I commenced to teach the letters of the alphabet and the first strokes of penmanship. It is not an easy task to teach scholars who do not commence their education till they are forty or fifty years of age ! It was plodding work indeed, and at first seemed almost hopeless. Those men and women, however, stuck to it, and it was our joy to see many of them able to read and write well. The governor was among the number of these, and though he was probably about sixty when he commenced, he persevered until he was able to read a psalm or a portion of the New Testament at our services. This was brought to the knowledge of the Queen, who sent him a letter of hearty congratulation, much to his delight.

" Teaching the children was a far less arduous task. A few months after our arrival we had 400 children in our schools and that number soon rose to over 1,200. When other duties permitted, I used to go to the school morning and afternoon, and no department of our varied work gave me more joy or greater encourage-ment. It was our custom to hold periodical examina-tions of our pupils and I will refer to one that was held four years after the commencement of our work.

" It was arranged that from our four principal stations, at each of which I had placed a native evangelist, six boys and three girls should be selected, and come up to Ambàtondrazàka, to join in a competitive examination with the same number of scholars from our central

school. One Monday morning found these forty-five
scholars seated in the classroom which I had built ;
that day and part of Tuesday they were examined in
arithmetic. They had to do a hundred sums, ranging
from simple addition up to multiplication of vulgar
fractions. The boy who took the first place did eighty-
nine correctly, and the first among the girls, eighty-five.
Then came spelling ; a hundred words up to five syllables. One little girl wrote ninety-nine words correctly ;
then followed four boys with ninety-eight. An examination in the four Gospels came next, and the first
place was taken by a lad whose answers were so excellent
that he obtained the maximum number of fifty marks.
On the Thursday morning they were examined in reading,
and I was much gratified by the fluency with which
they read out of an entirely new book.

" Grammar and geography were included in the
programme, but they did not distinguish themselves
in those subjects.

" I can unhesitatingly affirm that the people appreciated and profited by this part of our work, and great
was the love of the children for their schools. One
woman, whom Mrs. Pearse had taught to read and
write, forcibly expressed the benefits which she and her
companions had received, when she said, ' If you had not
come here, we should have been lost, we should still
have been as ignorant as the cattle on our plains ! '

" There were other pleasing incidents in connection
with this class. There was a young girl attracted by
the sewing ; after much hesitation, she was eventually
persuaded to enter the room, but in much fear and
trembling, for while her teacher kept the needle in her
hand, she herself kept her eyes on the door, to make
sure that there was a way of escape, if anything terrible

should happen ! She came back, however, next week ; in time went to school, became one of our best scholars, was sent up to Imèrina to the Girls' High School, and in the end married one of our teachers and so became associated with the work in the district.

" One woman said of the teaching, ' I like the reading, I like the writing, I like the arithmetic, but I like the Bible lesson best of all.'

" During four years I sold to the natives many publications in their own language. Besides monthly magazines, these included 320 Bibles, 672 Testaments, 590 Luke, 748 hymn books, 816 catechisms and 5,000 lessons.

" Further, the work of a doctor occupied much of my time among the Sihànaka. During the years I was with them, I saw and attended some 9,000 cases, not including many thousands of vaccinations and many tooth extractions. There have been occasions when my wrists have positively ached with pulling out tooth after tooth, in places where my visits were few and far between.

" One of the first and likewise one of the worst of my cases was that of a man whose name was Rafiringa, but whom we also referred to as Lazarus. He reached Ambàtondrazàka, a stranger and sick, about a year before us. His wife forsook him at an early stage of his illness and so he was left alone, among strangers. His disease grew so offensive that the inhabitants were no longer willing for him to share their huts, and he told me that once he lay in the open thoroughfare for four days and nights, when the dogs not only licked his sores, but he was in actual danger of being eaten by them. A few days after our arrival, I noticed the poor wretch crawl to the gateway of our compound and squat there, with a crowd around him. I was busy at the time and thinking him to be some poor idiot, I sent him a little bit of money with the request to go away.

"A few days after, however, I heard so much about his condition that I resolved to try and find him, and when I had succeeded, a more sad, wretched and revolting wreck of humanity I never beheld. Refused the use of a hut, he had crawled beneath the shelter of a mud wall, against which leaned a few stout rushes.

"Crouched there, with only a few rags upon him and with a cow-dung fire smouldering close beside him, was poor Lazarus; in appearance a human skeleton, but with just sufficient strength to hold out his hands in an imploring manner and whisper, 'I am lost, I am lost.' The sight was most affecting, while the stench from his putrid and open sores was quite overpowering. I felt that an effort must be made to do something for him, though he seemed already beyond human help. I succeeded in getting a few of the people sufficiently roused to erect a rude hut for him and then I took him in hand. Day after day, I went to that hut and washed and dressed his sores. We sent him cooked food from our kitchen, we got a mattress and some kind of clothing; we supplied him with medicines and, in a word, did everything we could to restore him to health. For weeks he wavered between life and death, but at length I was rewarded by noticing marked improvement in his condition. His sores showed a disposition to heal, flesh began to form on his bones, his strength gradually increased, from sitting up he was able to stand for a few minutes, then to walk a few steps, and finally to come as far as our house. Ultimately, by

God's blessing, poor Lazarus became quite well, only remaining a little lame in one leg. He afterwards regularly attended our Sunday services; he was the wonder of the place and became a living and walking advertisement of the doctor missionary."

CHAPTER VII

Work Amongst the Sihànaka
1875 to 1881

WE have realized to some extent the ignorance and degradation of the Sihànaka, and have had a rapid survey from Mr. Pearse's own pen of what he and Mrs. Pearse had striven to effect among them during the years they were working in their midst. There are still some details of the picture to be filled in, in order that we may obtain a true idea of the methods used to bring the gospel to the heathen.

Simplicity was the great characteristic of the work done. It was realized from the outset that the natives had enjoyed scarcely any civilizing influences and that there had been practically no foundations yet laid on which to build. True, there had been a native evangelist who had spent three years there, and there were some churches and even schools and congregations. But the churches were only built in deference to the supposed wishes of the Queen and the congregations only assembled for the same reason, indeed it was rumoured that occasionally even physical compulsion was employed in order to procure them at all. The teaching in the schools was described by Mr. Pearse as merely a make-believe. First of all, therefore, a foundation was necessary and, while by no means disregarding the hard task of teaching the adults, preaching to them, and trying to win them by medical care, it was the teaching of the children that was regarded all along as being the most promising mode of effecting the desired alteration in the district.

At first, five schools were started in the larger towns of Antsihànaka and 400 children came. The minds of the majority of the parents were full of suspicion and their dread of the probable effects of the teaching upon their children was great. The richer among them were even willing to distribute as much as a hundred dollars in bribing certain officials, so as to secure the exemption of their children. One church member was suspended for accepting such a bribe. One of the present evangelists in the district tells how these suspicions and animosities were overcome. In his journeyings about the district, Mr. Pearse made a point of trying to arrive at the houses of the dissentients somewhere about the meal time. Native hospitality demanded an invitation being given, which was forthwith accepted, and the missionary would sit on the floor with the native and partake of the same rice and greens ; they would talk about all manner of things and by degrees the suspicion would wane, and be succeeded by delight at this pleasant companion who had come among them ! Then the matter of the teaching and its advantages would be broached, and the dread lest the children should get to school be turned into a fear lest they might not ! There was the wisdom of the serpent and likewise the harmlessness of the dove !

Thus the schools were filled and the progress was wonderful. At the gatherings for presentation of prizes, the elders would be amazed at seeing little mites of seven or eight standing up and reading clearly and intelligibly out of their books. Satisfaction was general.

The missionary was rewarded, the parents were gratified and the children were educated. In due time some of the elder boys were sent out in their turn as teachers, and some were even sent up to Antanànarìvo to the High School or the College. The progress of the girls was quite as gratifying as that of the boys, and it was evident that the Sihànaka were by no means lacking in intelligence. Before Mr. Pearse left the district, the five schools had grown to eighteen, and the number of children, as he states in the last chapter, had risen to over 1,200.

A striking testimony to the value of the instruction given lies in the fact that at the present time almost all the Sihànaka now working in the government offices or holding responsible positions in the church were pupils under Mr. Pearse—all, that is, who are sufficiently old. This was remarked upon by no less an authority than General Gallieni. Such a result, however, did not come without toil and effort ; constant personal inspection and personal teaching were given ; visits were paid to the schools all over the district ; time, money and labour were spent freely in the endeavour to raise the Sihànaka by making life a larger and a better thing for them, so that gradually its full import might dawn upon them.

The work amongst the adults was of a very multifarious character. Everything that could possibly be done to gain an entrance for the gospel into their hearts was done, in so far as time permitted. But the requirements of so large a district could not possibly be met without much native assistance. Therefore the procedure adopted was that at each of the larger villages an evangelist was stationed, who should be responsible for the religious services on the Sundays, and, at that time, also for the teaching of the school on the weekdays ; he was to do all he could to give his fellow-villagers the benefit of his better education and enlighten-ment.

These evangelists were young men trained at the Theological College in Antanànarìvo ; they had done four years study, before commencing which they were required to give evidence of their spiritual qualification and genuine desire for such work, and they were under the scrutiny of their teachers during the whole course of their training. Of necessity a large amount of the responsibility for the missionary work in such large areas must devolve upon these men, and it is only in keeping with the general principle at work everywhere that the natives should be roused as far as possible to the duty of bringing Christianity to their fellow-countrymen. At the commencement of his work in Antsihànaka Mr. Pearse was assisted by five evangelists ; the one at the central station was appointed and supported by the Palace church, and though, in some cases, these men were not altogether amenable to the control of the missionary, this man appeared at first to be entirely trustworthy. The other four were appointed and supported by the London Missionary Society ; the arrangement was that the church was responsible for providing a house for him and his family to live in, and sufficient rice for their consumption, while a stipend of eight dollars (about thirty-two shillings) was paid monthly by the Society.

It was Mr. Pearse's custom to try and visit all his churches every two months ; from time to time he would, in addition, be away touring through the whole district for as long as a month at a time, sleeping wherever he could, in a schoolroom or sometimes in exceedingly filthy native huts. He was thus able to control the

work done by the evangelists and take a direct share,
by preaching, visiting and the holding of Bible classes,
in the endeavour to help the villagers. His reports
of the evangelists give them great credit for their
patience, wisdom and earnestness. He says, " I can
record the confidence I have in the genuineness of their
Christian characters, and the consistency of their
conduct. They manifest a humble and tractable
disposition and a consciousness of weakness and insufficiency for their work, which leads them to look up for
the wisdom and grace they need." Of one man
he says, " I was surprised and thankful to find the
efficient state into which he has brought his school,
and the order and attention of the congregation in
his church. He is doing *more*, and exerting a
greater influence for good, than could reasonably have
been expected." Some of them " suffered severely
from fever, but none of them," he says " has ever
hinted to me a desire to give up the work, or expressed
a wish to remove to a more healthy part of the island."

We shall find the central idea of Mr. Pearse's own
mode of working and of winning a way to the hearts of
the people in a sentence in one of his reports : " If we are
to reach them, *I am persuaded that more must be done
by going to them, and coming into personal contact with
them in their dwellings* "—a carrying out of the principle
adopted by Mr. Pearse with such eminent success in
Imèrina.

The present evangelist at Ambàtondrazàka bears
eloquent testimony to Mr. Pearse's wonderful powers of
adaptability to the people, in a paper which may be
freely translated as follows : " His manner, when visiting, was such as to put the people entirely at their ease,
neither was there anything to make them feel ashamed

in his presence.   He did not turn up his nose even at the
dirty houses nor their entire lack of comfort, for when he
entered, he just sat down, like a Malagasy, on the mat
that was always spread for the guest.   There was   no
careful protecting of his clothes, lest they might be
contaminated.   If it was a meal-time, he was always
ready to join them, however humble the meal might be.
One day he went into the house of a certain man with
a large family ; finding them all seated round the
tray eating sweet potato, he too sat down with them
and ate his share, talking with them the while.   When
they had finished he spoke to them of the love of God,
and of salvation, and urged them to pray and to come
to Him to be saved.   That man afterwards brought
his relations to Christ, and encouraged as many as he
could to unite in building a church, and as long as he
lived he was earnest in doing all in his power, in the
service of God.

" Another time he saw, on his travels, an old man
sitting sunning himself, so he joined him and tried to
get into conversation with him.   He told him of all the
progress that there now was and interested him im-
mensely in it all, so that the old man acknowledged
with marked approval what was being done, but added
that such as he were now too old to learn much but it
was the children who must receive this new learning.
All the old folk gathered round as soon as Mr. Pearse
had gone and listened to his delighted comments on
the talk he had enjoyed so much.   The upshot was that
they sent the children in such numbers to the school
that it soon became one of the largest in the whole
district.

" In these ways he gained the confidence of the
Sihànaka and they were willing to talk freely with him,

thus he was able to help them and draw them upward, they were even willing to reveal themselves to him and obtain his sympathy, because they looked up to him as to a father who had no wish to humble them.

" But if he saw anything, either in the behaviour of the people or the state of their houses, that was not as it should be, he did not hesitate to direct and counsel them and he had a wonderful faculty of doing this without offending them.

" He did not spare himself or consider his own fatigue, for his love for the Malagasy was so great, and so great too his desire for their salvation, that he was willing to run many risks in his work for them. Sometimes when he was ready to start out for his meetings, the bearers did not turn up ; sometimes it was raining so hard that, although they had come, they would not carry him. Then off he went by himself, carrying his umbrella and his bag so as to be in time for his meeting, where he arrived, in due course, often wet through, with his clothes all bespattered with mud from slipping on the dreadful paths. Three times he and his men were almost drowned in crossing the rivers. Once on going over one of the bridges, which consisted merely of a log thrown over the stream, the log turned over while he was crossing and he fell into the water, which at that spot swarmed with crocodiles. Four men immediately jumped in too, so as to frighten away the crocodiles with their noise, and then all swam to the shore. This story made a great impression, and on arriving home, he had to receive congratulatory visits from many of the people, including the governor, who solemnly forbade his going out during the wet season ! It was not only the sermons that Mr. Pearse was so well able to deliver that charmed their ears, his whole life was a sermon, and this made the people so eager to listen to his preaching.   When he visited a village he used to say to the people, ' If there are any of you who wish to give up your idols and pray to the true God, do not be afraid, for the Holy Spirit is much stronger than the idols and can help you by His continual presence, and the idols will not be able to do you any harm.'   He did not show disrespect to or rudely ignore the feelings of the people concerning the idols.   One day an evangelist was very scornful of the idols, and derided the people for believing in them.   Immediately afterwards he stumbled and broke his leg !   The occasion was used for a little good advice about the methods to be used for enlightening the people's ignorance, not by temper but by patient endeavour.

" He was never harsh, but all was in order and done with perfect gentleness; at the same time he was firm and would not give way merely to obtain the goodwill of people.   What was right he adhered to, irrespective of consequences.   Once one of his evangelists, whom he had trusted implicitly, was charged with gross immorality.   Though grieved beyond measure, he tried at first to obtain a confession from the man, but without success.   On further investigation he obtained absolute proofs and brought the case before the church. The church however, being under the influence of the accused, took his part and refused to disown him.   After doing all he could to bring about a satisfactory termination, Mr. Pearse finally went the length of closing the church, and going up to Antanànarìvo to get a settlement.   When he returned, supported by the authority of all he had consulted, he found the people very antagonistic, but by his forbearance and wisdom and the greatness of his love he won them over.   The

SIHÀNAKA MEN.

church finally gave way entirely, and asked his pardon for their behaviour, confessing that they had been afraid on account of the high position of the offender.

" The many churches built in Antsihànaka are a witness to the devotion and diligence of Mr. Pearse in furthering the Kingdom of God here, and although only a few of these churches are now standing, the work of the gospel is very far from being dead ; the people often refer to the worshipping in those churches and some of them long for the rebuilding of such places of worship amongst them.   On account of all that Mr. Pearse did, and of the beauty of his character his fame here is great, and the people very frequently mention his name, because they regard it as so sweet."

The medical work done by Mr. Pearse in Antsihànaka made a very great impression.   That it was absolutely necessary to undertake it, is evident when we remember that the natives had no medical attendants worthy of the name.   He says, " Men and women who are recognized by the natives as doctors are common in all parts of Madagascar, but these have no acquaintance with anatomy or knowledge of diseases and they are altogether ignorant of either the medical or the hygienic treatment proper for the sick.   They employ powerful purgatives and various native vegetable infusions ; they use vapour baths of a rude kind ; they insist that the patient must consume an undiminished quantity of food ; and, although utterly unable to diagnose disease, they always give a favourable prognosis.   The fees which they demand are not inconsiderable, and money, cloth, poultry and even oxen come pretty freely into their hands.   By the more intelligent and educated natives they are held in deserved contempt, but the ignorant masses place implicit confidence in them

8

and carry out their instructions most scrupulously, especially in those districts where the power of charms and witchcraft is still acknowledged."

Realizing this crying need for medical work, Mr. Pearse made a definite attempt to supply the natives with something more trustworthy. He examined patients twice a week, but was of course willing to see those in real need, at other times. He promised with God's blessing to do all he could for them, though he told them that he had no elixir of life. He tried his best to get the people to really follow the advice given and finally he urged those who, by God's mercy, were cured, to make what contribution they could to the cost of the medicines.

There was a very large response to this effort. People overcame their scruples and consulted the white man, and some even went so far as to announce that their doing so was the result of a favourable divination! Visits from about 9,000 individuals were registered during the six years, but these did not include a large number of vaccinations and tooth extractions. Small-pox was formerly a great scourge in Madagascar, but after vaccination was seriously undertaken, its ravages became much less common, until at the present time it is confined to parts of the island where systematic vaccination has not been undertaken.

In the extraction of teeth Mr. Pearse attained a wonderful facility, and his skill was taken full advantage of. He says of his patients, " they seldom make a scene or even utter a cry ; one little boy was an exception, he winced and cried a little, but the moment the tooth was out, he jumped from his chair and stroked my shoulders and chest, saying, ' Thank you, O friend ; thank you, O friend ! ' "

Opportunities came in abundance of using the medical work to further the spread of the gospel, and as Mr. Pearse himself testified, " the frequent personal contact with the sick and their friends has given us opportunity to speak of spiritual things, which otherwise we should not have enjoyed and, in some cases, we are able to recognize that religious benefit has been received." The story of Lazarus, already related in the last chapter, is an excellent example of the devotion with which this work was carried on, and this case naturally made a deep impression, especially so as it was practically the first act in the establishment of the Mission in Antsi-hànaka. It is interesting to find it alluded to by the evangelist, whose paper has been quoted above. He says: " He spent no end of trouble over that poor man, for every day he went himself to wash the sores and dress them, going even two or three times a day to see him. The people were amazed to see Mr. Pearse turn up his sleeves and set to work, not showing disgust at the job, but doing all he did as if the man were his dearest friend. By God's blessing the man recovered, but Mr. Pearse was not satisfied with curing him and letting him go, for he crowned his work by giving him seven dollars in order to start him with a stall at a little market, where he could gain an honest livelihood."

Another evangelist, who worked with him at this time, writes : " Whenever he came to the place of worship he would first of all go round and shake hands with all the people already assembled ; all their names he knew, not just ten or twenty people but a large number, men, women and children. That established very happy relationships between him and them, and these were the foundations upon which he built. His preaching was in plain and simple language ; abstruse thought and difficult illustrations he avoided. With his direct speech he made everything so clear that it was impossible for the people to avoid giving their assent to what he said. While he was preaching, everything about him helped the impression he was trying to make : the brightness of his eyes, the outspread hands, the warmth of his heart, the very shaking of his hair, all gave pleasure to the audience, and made them the more ready to listen to him. He had thirty-three churches under his charge in Antsihànaka, all but a few of which he himself founded.

" He was much interested in helping the grown-up people to learn to read ; those who wished to learn were handed over to the care of those who could already read, and these had classes of two or three or even up to ten ; and such was the spirit of emulation among these teachers that they very soon had their pupils able to read the Scriptures.

" He was very successful with his Bible classes and used to combine the churches near one another for the purposes of these ; difficult passages he tried to translate into Sihànaka dialect, so that they might be quite understood. Every three months he used to go round to visit the churches ; the first thing he did was to visit the people from house to house, and often enough the feet of the evangelist who accompanied him, ached again with trying to keep up with him in these visits. Simple homely talks about the love of God and salvation through Jesus Christ were the feature of these times, but as he went about he tried to help the people all he could in what pertained to their bodily welfare, as well as their spiritual. His wise advice, given under the influence of the Holy Spirit, was incontrovertible, unless by those who were too hard-hearted or ignorant to pay attention to it. Thus he was often able to give most valuable help in disagreements, whether between husband and wife or different members of a family or community. An example of his consideration for the people is to be found in his refusal of such gifts of food as were customary from the churches to officials on their travels ; he knew that such gifts were presented from a sense of duty rather than from affection and he would not add an iota to their burdens. But go to their houses and eat with them, yes, that was something quite different !

" The school examinations were occasions marked by great enthusiasm, and when they were finished the prizes were well worth receiving ; he gave the scholars their choice of books, such as Bibles, Testaments, or hymn books, or pictures and beads. The first in each village would get a Bible, and either a dollar or else a garment ; these prizes were given with no niggardly hand, and that generosity was a feature of all Mr. Pearse's work.

" In his work among the sick he had great opportunities of showing his love to the Sihànaka. One of his favourite sayings used to be, ' Love knows how to take pains,' and on the strength of that he was willing to do anything for them, walking out to the villages round about to visit them, because there were no bearers, or else putting up with the jolting of the Sihànaka bearers, unused to carrying the palanquin.

" There was a leper boy in Ambàtondrazàka in such a repulsive condition that his own people would not have anything to do with him. Mr. Pearse took him up and did everything for him, washing his sores, giving him food and clothing, and even putting up for him a little house near his own. There he used to attend to him, and while others looked on, disgusted with the sights and smells, he bore them all without a murmur. He outdid even the Good Samaritan !

" There was a boy in the first class of our school who went out early one morning to take the birds he had snared. The snare is laid in the evening and emptied in the morning. Early in the morning like that, the crocodiles are still on the banks, as they do not go out into the deeper water till the sun is well up and the water warmed. This boy was excited over the birds and did not notice the crocodile near, until it was upon him. He was seized by the leg, and though fortunately not dragged into the water, it took nearly all the men in the village to release him and kill the beast. That day Mr. Pearse happened to come to teach, so the parents told him what had occurred and he went off at once and with quick steps hurried to the boy. He washed the leg and bound it up and did all that he could, but his advice to the parents was to hurry up to the capital with the boy as quickly as possible and he would bear all expenses.

" Various things he did to help the Sihànaka. He found that a certain big market held on Mondays prevented many people from coming to church. The market at Ambàtondrazàka was on Saturday, and this other market a day's journey to the north was on Monday, so the merchants would move on from the one to the other, travelling on Sunday and so neglecting their souls to fill their purses. After representations to the governor, this market was changed to Thursday and the merchants had no further excuse for not coming to church.

" The cultivation of rice and sugar-cane was a great source of wealth to the Sihànaka, but the sugar-cane was used for making rum which ruined them, body and soul. So, after much thought and prayer, he decided to teach the natives to make sugar instead, as sugar was very dear, because it had to be imported from Imèrina. Then the cane was put to a proper use and the prosperity of the province increased proportionately.

" He introduced also the cultivation of silkworms, and encouraged the people to devote their attention to that. The mulberries flourished amazingly, and so without difficulty the people found a new opening for gain."

A strange insight was often obtained into Sihànaka superstitions. " One morning," Mr. Pearse says, " I was surprised to notice patient after patient come in with a single grain of Indian corn tied round the neck, which I learnt was a charm for averting evil. It was reported that a tenrec (an animal like a large hedgehog) having been so unfortunate as to be caught, had volunteered valuable information on the condition that its life should be spared. ' There is a black thing,' it said, ' a disease, which will come from the west and kill many people, therefore let everyone wear a grain of Indian corn, for that will prove a certain talisman.' " On another occasion " a dog had announced that a hurricane, causing grievous famine, would devastate the district ; that immense hailstones would descend and that even the very heavens would fall. To prevent this calamity the people were told to get six black and six white beads and wear them round the neck."

" Among those who came to the dispensary one day was an old man who wore around his neck a greasy string upon which were threaded two black and two white beads. I asked him the object of wearing them, on hearing which question he put up his hand to the string and it broke. ' Oh,' he said, ' it is of no further use now, for she told me as much (' she ' being a certain sorceress). She said we must wear it to cause the rains to fall, and we did ; so the rains did come last year, but if we had not obeyed her, there would have been a drought.' "

Mr. Pearse was ever ready by means of simple medicines and simple operations to alleviate all the sickness that he could and to wean the natives from such senseless superstitions and charms. The work, however, was no little tax upon his strength, as the superintendence of so large a district, with such crying needs, was very arduous. There was no pretension to elaborate methods, but there was knowledge and a sort of medical genius, a great love of order, a readiness to find the simplest way of doing things, and to economize time ; by means of these a very valuable contribution to medical missionary work in Madagascar was made. As noted above, no stated charge was made for medicine or advice ; and many others would have found it very difficult to obtain any contributions whatsoever to the cost of medicine ; but Mr. Pearse's persuasiveness was always equal to the task, and he was able to impress his patients with such a sense of the duty they owed to the source of their recovery, that though the amount raised was not at all sufficient to defray the total expenses, it formed a substantial contribution thereto. In one year, £6 was given, in another £11, all made up of amounts varying from one to five dollars down to a few pence. The rest of the cost of the medical work was defrayed by donations from friends in England, whose names often figure in Mr. Pearse's reports, with appropriate and grateful allusions to their kindness. There were not a few friends whose contributions enabled him to assist needy churches and needy individuals with handsome gifts. The gratitude of the patients was also shown in their bringing such things as fowls, geese, eggs and fruit as presents, and sometimes they prayed fervently for the divine blessing to rest on their benefactors.

There are not wanting the usual incidents of a diverting character, which now and again serve to relieve the monotony of such work as his. On one occasion, chancing to take shelter from the rain in a wayside hut, he found one of his patients living there. Mr. Pearse thus describes the incident: " On my asking after the patient, a friend informed me that she was still ill, but he assured me emphatically that her medicine was well taken care of. He took down a basket and, with evident satisfaction, showed me the bottle, still full of medicine as it had been received from me three months before." It had been preserved as a charm, instead of being taken! " How hard it has sometimes been to secure the carrying out of the treatment! I gave one woman a medicine in powder, telling her to take the weight of two grains of unhusked rice thrice daily. As the Malagasy at that time were accustomed to cut up their dollars into tiny pieces and to pay these out, according to their weight in the small scales which everyone carried, this was a very usual way of ordering medicines. This woman, however, had taken the medicine and swallowed the weights (in rice grains) as well! "

Mr. Pearse closes a paper on his medical work by saying, " It has given me opportunities of speaking of spiritual disease and telling of the Great Physician. By it, pain has been relieved, suffering has been alleviated, disease has been cured, and life has, in some instances, been lengthened. Hereby sorrow has been lessened, while joy has been increased. For such

results who would not be glad ? Who would not give
heartfelt thanks to God ? ''

The difficulties incident to the superstitions and
ignorance of the Sihànaka have often been mentioned.
Their rum-drinking has been alluded to also. In one
small village no less than a hundred stills were counted
for the manufacture of the stuff, and on one occasion
when the children at the school were questioned as to
whether they were accustomed to drink it, it was found
that there were very few indeed of them who had not
taken it in larger or smaller quantities and with greater
or less frequency.

The almost universal lying and the very frequent
examples of hypocrisy met with proved great difficulties
to the missionary in Antsihànaka. It was almost
impossible sometimes to detect these evils, so clever
were the people in disguising them.

Other difficulties of a different character confronted
Mr. Pearse. The marshes in which Antsihànaka
abounded bred enormous numbers of mosquitoes, and
the malaria due to these not only brought its own
quota of patients for treatment, but the missionary
and his family were frequently among the victims.
The repeated attacks of fever told greatly on the health
of all the members of the family and necessitated their
seeking from time to time healthier conditions at Antanànarìvo, where at that time there was no malaria.
The persistency of this fever when one is out of health
is intensely trying, for the attacks come daily or every
other day, often in spite of quinine, and reduce the
patient to a state of great feebleness. The consequent
strain and anxiety to a missionary, working all alone,
as he was, were intense ; no other white man within
a hundred miles ; and himself, on whom his dear ones

had to rely for treatment, liable to be utterly incapacitated at any time. Of all this, Mr. Pearse had his due share and more.

The state of his family's health, coupled with the exigencies of the mission at the time, pointed to the advisability of transferring his services to the mission to the Bètsilèo to the south of the central province, and thus Mr. Pearse's connection with Antsi-hànaka terminated during the earlier part of 1881. Foundations had been laid, difficulties had been success-fully met and were being overcome, education was proceeding in a most encouraging way, and some im-pression was being made on the degraded life of the natives. Statistically, the results were satisfactory, and there was certainly evidence of the teaching having really penetrated the hearts of many of those, who had been during these years the objects of so much careful and faithful labour on the part of Mr. and Mrs. Pearse.

He likens the state of affairs to a sight that once met his gaze : " When returning from my recent journey and, while we were yet on the higher land, before descending to the level of the lake, we opened the tent door on Saturday morning to find ourselves enveloped in a very thick, heavy mist, which con-tinued to surround us for nearly two hours after we left the village where we passed the night. The sun had risen to some height above the horizon, but its influences were not felt. Between the king of day above and darkness around us there seemed to be a contest as to who should reign that day. Now when a break appeared, it looked as though the sun would assert its rightful sway ; while anon, when thicker clouds of mist surrounded us, it seemed that darkness had gained

the victory.   About nine o'clock, however, all doubt was
at an end, for in its full beauty and power the sun shone
forth ; mists flew away to the far west, and were seen
no more, while there seemed to be joy around us and
gladness in every object of nature.   My thoughts
dwelt upon our work ; and in what had passed I saw a
similitude of what is taking place among the Sihànaka."

CHAPTER VIII

The Bètsilèo Province and People
1881 to 1886

THE Bètsilèo province is a well-watered and mountainous region about 200 miles long by 50 miles wide, the capital of which, Fianàrantsòa, is situated some 200 miles south of Antanànarìvo. The physical conditions to a large extent reproduce those of Imèrina but while the heat is somewhat less intense, there is very great fertility in some parts of the province.

The inhabitants are a quite different tribe from the Hova and much more negroid in character. They are darker, have broader noses, woolly hair, very little beard and are of larger build than the Hova. Though credited with lack of intelligence, they show a marked superiority over the Hova in natural artistic capacity, and ornament their houses, beds and tombs with carving, which sometimes has quite an elaborate appearance. Their houses, at the time of which we are writing, were low huts built of wood, bulrushes or banana stems, thatched with rush and plastered; they were built facing the west, and had two openings, both at a height of about two and a half feet, so that, as one missionary states, it was difficult for a tall man to make a dignified entrance! There were shelves round two sides, sometimes in three tiers, to satisfy certain superstitious requirements; each house also contained hearth, water pot and bedstead. They were frequently very much overcrowded and very dirty, and their condition as to cleanliness was not improved by the occupants having their fowls and calves in the house with them, though fortunately they drew the line at pigs, in which respect they showed another trait of superiority over some of the Hova. They formerly built villages, protected against invasion by deep ditches, thick hedges of prickly pear and a narrow entrance ; now, however, there are to be found many scattered homesteads, consisting of three or four houses, surrounded by a circular mud wall or hedge of cactus or thorns.

The clothing of the Bètsilèo was meagre, consisting of lamba and loin-cloth and sometimes, in the case of the women, of a coarse rush mat wrapped round them. There was little tendency towards ornament, though some wore broad necklaces and anklets and perhaps a couple of silver bracelets on each arm. Their hair was plaited and then arranged in rounded, flattened knobs all over the head, with a silver ring dangling behind; much time was expended over the performance, but at rare intervals, and one woman would spend nearly a day in doing the hair of another for a remuneration of twopence !

The occupations of the men were the various outdoor duties, such as tending oxen, building, planting and attending generally to their ricefields, while the women fetched water, did the cooking, were responsible for such tidying and cleaning as the house received, and spent time in weaving and plaiting.

There appeared but little that was elevating in the contemplation of this tribe, but further study of them revealed many points of great interest, both in their customs and beliefs. They were a people of few words,

and uncouth both in language and demeanour ; not
attractive, not sharp-witted and not by any means
the equals of the Hova in capacity for bargaining and
business transactions generally. They have proved,
however, to be as capable of receiving instruction as the
Hova, and their children reach as high a standard as
do those in Imèrina. They were united by strong clan
and family feelings, but were much given to quarrels
and litigation, and though less cunning and less immoral
than some other tribes, they were untrustworthy,
insincere and intemperate. Their clannishness proved
a difficulty when churches had to be built or teachers
placed, as they were very much less disposed to act in
conjunction with members of other clans than with their
own.

Like all the Malagasy tribes the Bètsilèo acknowledge
a supreme Being, but of Him they appeared to know very
little. The position that should have been taken by
His worship was occupied by tradition and superstition ;
it was the ancestral spirits who were supposed to be
responsible for the various happenings on earth. They
held the doctrine of transmigration of souls, and believed
that the spirits of their chiefs inhabited the bodies of
certain serpents, those of lesser dignitaries became
crocodiles, while the ordinary tribesman turned into some
fearsome creature of the imagination, somewhat
reminiscent of a skeleton.

Holding these ideas, they naturally paid great reverence to the serpents, and took vengeance on anyone in-
juring them. On the appearance of such a serpent they
endeavoured to find out its identity by noticing the
direction it took, and there were great rejoicings when
its propitious presence settled amongst them. Crocodiles
also it was considered very wrong to kill. Their lives

were made miserable by their dread of the evil influence of their ghostly ancestors and of witchcraft, and it is thus very easy to see why they should pay much attention to the words of those who were supposed to have knowledge of the occult, and pay much honour also to their persons. The diviner was a very great and important personage ; he really appears to have frequently been an observant individual, who retained in his memory much that he had seen or heard, and was aware of many family secrets ; and, being accustomed to speak in a very oracular manner, he easily obtained credit for extraoidinary wisdom. The mysteries of counting out the beans and arranging them in various ways, from which the reply to each consultation was supposed to be deduced, were watched with much awe. Then the cause of the evil which had befallen them was stated and the steps necessary to remove it were indicated, these steps being often of an involved character, so that infringement thereof was probable and a loophole thus provided to explain any lack of success that might follow the procedures.

The diviner was not above putting down the misfortune to the presence of a moth, which he proceeded to look for, and, after slily liberating one that he had brought with him, he would make supreme efforts to catch it and obtain much applause for his discernment !

Sickness was accounted for on the supposition that the unfortunate individual had unwittingly collided with a ghost in the dark, or that he had been bewitched, or that his spirit had left his body. These misfortunes were suitably treated ; various potions were administered ; his bed was moved or his unfortunate body hustled about to bring back the spirit. Charms were used against mishaps and seem to have been so implicitly believed in,

as to render quite unnecessary the dictates of common-
sense ; they were either worn on the person or kept in
the house. Vaccination on the forehead and limbs would
ward off lightning ; on the approach of locusts they did
not, as is the custom elsewhere, light fires so as to smoke
out the invaders, but they simply employed their charms
and awaited the result ; on crossing a stream they
addressed the crocodiles, and to rid their houses of vermin
they wrapped up some rice in a leaf, placed it at some
distance away and invited the pests to kindly follow !

They recognized also very many taboos, which were
studiously observed. One clan would not use a canoe,
so on arriving at the river, the bearers laid their goods
on the top of a waterpot and carried them across by
propelling that.

The diviners were consulted before embarking on any
undertaking of importance, such as building a house,
going a journey, marrying a wife, and they could obtain
from them charms to use against childlessness or drought ;
and in order to ensure success in any nefarious proceedings they might be contemplating.

Offerings were made after the success of a project and
sacred stones were anointed. On eating rice also a small
portion was thrown on to the shelves for the spirits of
ancestors or slaves inhabiting there or sometimes for
the deity himself.

The most surprising feature about their burial customs
was the fact that interment did not take place for months,
from three months to a year elapsing before the body
was buried. During the interval there was much in-
terference with all labour going on in the neighbourhood, and as rum circulated freely, the disturbance
of the public peace was disgraceful.

During the funeral ceremonies the ancestors were

propitiated, and were requested to prevent the spirit of the departed from wandering about and causing annoyance to the living. The home of departed spirits was supposed to be a gorge in the east of Bètsilèo, from which proceeded from time to time weird sounds, probably actually produced by the rushing of wind in narrow valleys, but attributed by the natives to the cries of the ghosts.

Over the graves were often erected solid squares of stone and the skulls of the cattle killed during the proceedings were ranged round the edges of these tombs.

Certain lucky stones and ancestral tombs were held in honour, the former being smeared as petitions were uttered, and the latter resorted to during illness, as it was supposed that the illness had been induced by stepping on this grave and would last until suitable restitution had been made to the offended spirit.

The Bètsilèo paid great reverence to age, and the possession of a long beard was a passport to their respect. They, as a rule, prevented the growth of hair on the face by plucking it out, but before a youth began to do so he had to pay sixpence to his father!

Bètsilèo is divided into four districts, the inhabitants of which show distinct tribal differences; these districts were under separate political supervision, and the same arrangement was found suitable on the commencement of mission work there. There were a few Christians at Fìanàrantsòa even in the days of the persecution, some Christian soldiers having settled there and some of the persecuted also fleeing there for refuge. On the death of the persecuting Queen, these no longer met in secret, but were able to unite for worship and in time formed a church, and such was their success that before long a second and then a third church had to be built.

The London Missionary Society had contemplated the founding of a mission settlement at Fìanàrantsòa and visits were paid by Mr. Jukes and Mr. Toy, in which the needs of the district were examined and other places also noted which promised to be suitable centres for work. In 1870, the mission was started but there was a great hindrance to success in the fact that most of the missionaries sent down there stayed only a comparatively short time. Much good work was done, and foundations were laid, but, from that and other causes, in some departments there was such a lack of progress, that in 1881 an entire change of staff in the town of Fìanàrantsòa was advised ; Mr. Pearse was invited down from the Antsihànaka mission, and two junior colleagues, Mr. Huckett and Mr. Johnson, recently arrived from England, were associated with him. Two brethren, stationed in other districts of Bètsilèo, Mr. Brockway in the north at Ambòsitra and Mr. Rowlands in the south at Ambòhimandròso, stayed on in charge of these districts. As the result of work done during the previous eleven years, the condition of the native Bètsilèo was a trifle better than has been described at the commencement of this chapter ; some light had penetrated their gross darkness, the seeds of education had been scattered and had brought some fruition and the people had become more accustomed to the presence of the European and consequently stood rather less in dread of him.

The disadvantages under which the work had been labouring could not fail to deeply impress Mr. Pearse when he was called upon to transfer his services from a flourishing station to one which was so much the reverse. He arrived at Fìanàrantsòa early in July, 1881, and after some examination of the district of Isàndra which

had been allotted to him, wrote to the Directors as
follows :—

"23rd January, 1882.

" The state of the London Missionary Society's mission
in the district is such as would make any Christian worker
sad. To me, who have been called away from a far
more promising work to take up that in this district,
it is a heavy burden of sorrow   *Nothing* is in a satisfactory condition, and *not one* department of the work
is promising or hopeful. Much, very much rather,
would I have commenced an entirely new work on quite
a new field, than have entered upon this. But your
voice in requesting me to come here was most distinct
and decided, and if this is the work which the Master
would have me to do, I am prepared to devote my fullest
energies to it ; and, God helping me, and with His Spirit
poured out, the work will yet be successful."

He was very much pained at the competition existing
between the London Missionary Society and that of
the Norwegians. It would have been his wish for the
land to be divided between these Protestant societies,
and distinct spheres of influence apportioned to each,
so as to avoid overlapping, waste of energy and confusion
in the minds of the heathen. To this point he recurs
again and again and it was to him one of the chief
problems to be settled, before prosecuting the work in
the Bètsilèo province to which he and his colleagues had
been called. As we proceed, we shall see that many
years were to elapse and much patience was to be exhausted before any such amicable arrangement could be
carried out.

He was glad to be able to qualify this adverse report
by enlarging on further discoveries of a more encouraging character, which he does in the following terms :—

" I am very happy to state that I have found the condition of the London Missionary Society Mission in the N. Sandra district decidedly better than that of S. Sandra. The chapels are not in such a ruinous condition ; the teachers in the schools have higher abilities ; and the attainments of some of the children are in advance of anything I found in South Sandra.

" The work at Kàlamavòny, our most western station, is in a flourishing condition. The chapel is a large and really good and substantial sun-dried brick building, and the congregation on the two occasions on which I have visited the place has been over a thousand. The condition of chapel, school and congregation is a very striking and pleasing contrast to the general state of things in Bètsilèo. Neither the Roman Catholics nor the Norwegians have been able to obtain any footing. The London Missionary Society chapel was built more than ten years ago by the natives, and, on account of the remote position of Kàlamavòny the work from the commencement has received no other personal over-sight from the missionary in charge than an occasional visit. Its singularly flourishing condition is therefore the more remarkable."

The work in which Mr. Pearse was engaged was very similar in character to that which he had left ; preaching, Bible classes, education, visiting, building and medical work filled his days. He was given the charge of a dispensary, in which excellent work was done. He quaintly says in a letter : " This morning I went out to hold a preachers' class at seven, but was stopped outside the schoolroom by a man who wanted to know if I could pull out a back tooth for his wife, as she was distracted with toothache. ' Oh, yes,' I said, and so off we went

to our little dispensary and had the tooth out before I
went to my preachers' class."

Some of the difficulties in connection with education
are brought out in the following letter extracted from
the *Chronicle.* " The Hova Governor of Fìanàrantsòa
is an old friend of mine, and when I returned from
inspecting the state of the mission in the Sandra district,
I called upon him and we had a lengthy conversation
about the very unsatisfactory state of things which
I found. Whether as the result of that conversation
or not I cannot say, but he has taken up the matter
of schools in a very practical manner. Officers of
the government have recently been sent through the
entire district to look into the number of scholars in
the existing schools, to make notes of those among
them who are adults and unfit to be scholars (this
with a view of their being removed), and also to place
new scholars in the schools. They have also publicly
announced a standard of education, upon reaching
which the children are to be free to leave the schools
in the future, instead of thinking (as they have done in
the past) that once in the schools, they are scholars
for ever. This standard is low, and will ultimately
be raised ; but it was most desirable that it should
be such as can be reached by some of the children
soon, in order that the present bad feelings entertained
by many of the parents against education may be
removed by seeing the children free after having been
educated.

" For more than a month previously my time was
spent in the Sandra districts, accompanying the members
of the local government, who have been placing new
scholars in the various mission schools.

" I will briefly describe the proceedings at one centre,

which will give some idea as to how the work of putting a large number of scholars into the schools has been carried out.

" The centre at which the people were to assemble was a village called Ikòlo. The London Missionary Society has a rudely-built mud chapel there, and another near. The Norwegians have six and the Roman Catholics three chapels within the radius which embraced the people assembled.

" In an open space near our chapel, a large mass of people were assembled, awaiting the arrival of the Queen's messengers. The chief messenger and those who accompanied him approached the spot in military order, preceded by a native band. After they had halted, the people gathered round them in a great circle ; the Sovereign was saluted in the usual Malagasy fashion, inquiries after her health and the welfare of the kingdom were made by a representative of the people and then the ' Queen's speech ' was delivered. In this the people were thanked for coming together and were assured that the Queen was seeking nothing but their welfare. The decisions about the scholars and their standard, already referred to, were then announced and explained. The scholars were required to possess either a Bible or a New Testament before leaving the schools.

" By the time this speech was delivered and replied to, the sun was low in the horizon and the assembly broke up. Early the next morning the work of receiving the new scholars was proceeded with. To leave it to the freewill of the people as to whether they would have their children taught or not would bring but a very limited number into the schools, so that some kind of ' Compulsory Education Act ' has had to be considered and carried out by the local government. For political purposes the Bètsilèo are sub-divided into small parties varying in number from twenty-five to one hundred, with a man at the head. It has been made compulsory for parents in each part to put into the schools children corresponding in number to their party. It was left to the parents to decide whether their children should learn with the London Missionary Society, Norwegian Missionary Society or the Roman Catholics, with the result that the figures of the respective missions were 15,211, 4,382 and 4,484.

" I hope for great things from this movement. It will give new life to our schools and we shall get a total of not less than 5,000 new scholars."

In a letter to some young friends at Lewes, Mr. Pearse describes a Christmas. He says: " At eight o'clock on Christmas morning, a service was held at each of our three chapels in this town, lasting about an hour, after which the people who had formed the congregations, and very many others, walked to an enclosure belonging to the Queen, about a mile away from the town, and there we held a united open-air service and I preached to a great crowd from that beautiful text in John iii. 16: ' God so loved the world that He gave His only begotten son,' etc. At the close of the service we were invited by the natives to a meal, consisting of turkeys, fowls, rice and fruit.

"We reached our home somewhat tired and scorched about three o'clock, and had the pleasure of finding that a mail from England had arrived during our absence and our Christmas joy was heightened by being able to read 'good news' of many relations and friends, who are very dear to us but from whom we are so far separated. The postman does not visit us every day in this part of the world, but only once a month."

The time of the first French war was rapidly approaching and though neither Fìanàrantsòa, nor in fact, any place in the interior of Madagascar was actually the scene of hostilities, it was inevitable but that there should be a very considerable amount of disturbance felt. Brief entries in Mr. Pearse's diary are of interest as showing how these developments affected the mission and himself personally. The decision had been come to that Mrs. Pearse should leave for England early in June, 1883, but this arrangement, as we shall see, was frustrated at the last moment.

" *June 1st.*—Started off six men in the morning with part of our luggage for Antanànarìvo. At prayer meeting in the evening we were told that a letter had been received stating that hostilities were on the eve of commencing.

" *2nd.*—Continued our preparations for leaving on Monday. In the afternoon the men left with our bedding and part of our provisions, to stay for us at our stopping place on Monday night.

" *3rd, Sunday.*—Called on the governor at the close of the morning service. He confirmed the information received. In the evening we conferred with our fellow missionaries as to the course we should pursue and decided to wait a day or two for further information.

" *4th, Monday.*—The men came according to appointment early in the morning. I told them to come again to-morrow. About ten o'clock a special messenger arrived from Antanànarìvo giving us information. In the afternoon we held a special committee meeting and it was decided that we stay in Fìanàrantsòa for the present.

" 6th.—Heard late in the evening that the government messengers had arrived bringing official information of the attack of the French on the west coast, and ordering all French subjects to leave by next Monday.

" 7th.—Great excitement in the town. About eight o'clock the officers went to the premises of the Roman Catholics, and delivered the royal message. We were sent for to the *róva* and had an official letter read to us recommending us to be in one town and promising all possible protection. The French have been selling off during the day.

" 11th, *Monday*.—Great excitement among the people from the early morning. I started to go to the dispensary as usual, but going towards the town I was met by soldiers coming from the *róva* (palace) towards the Catholic premises, and so I returned. About nine, the officers and more soldiers came down, and about ten all the French subjects, some fifteen men and four women, left on foot and commenced the journey to Mànanjàra. They intended to have had bearers but the men struck for higher wages at the last moment, and so they started on foot, leaving their palanquins and luggage behind.

" 13th.—The three thousand Bètsilèo recently enrolled as soldiers have been called up, and are now practising daily in the royal premises.

" 17th, *Sunday*.—Early this morning heard that messengers had arrived last evening, who brought word that spearmen were to be appointed to go from here towards Tamatàve, and that all the people are to arm and have liberty to buy guns and ammunition. The peace of Sunday has been somewhat disturbed.

" 25th.—All the teachers summoned by the governor and told that the boys must learn spear and shield drill. The natives do not forget to pray for their enemies.

" *Sunday, 22nd July.*—Government messengers arrived just as our morning service closed, bringing the sad news that Rànavàlona II. died at Antanànarìvo on Friday, 13th."

Mr. Pearse wrote : " The excitement among the Bètsilèo is not so great as that manifested by the Hova, and up to the present time we feel no anxiety for our personal safety among them. Our congregations in the town are at present unaffected."

In the month of August it became possible for Mrs. Pearse to take the journey to the coast, the route taken being the direct one to Mànanjàra on the east coast, and not the much longer *via* Antanànarìvo. The following letter to the Directors is of interest describing the experiences connected with leaving Madagascar ; Mr. Pearse escorted the party as far as Mauritius.

" Mànanjàra,
" *5th September*, 1883.

" The letter from the Rev. A. S. Huckett will inform you how that on the receipt of a letter from here, I was encouraged by the Committee to leave Fìanàrantsòa with Mrs. Pearse and our three children, in hope of catching the *Kroo Boy*, and overtaking Mr. Cousins and Mr. and Mrs. Briggs in Mauritius. We received that letter at mid-day on Wednesday, 15th August, and made our preparations for leaving Fìanàrantsòa, and travelled here in the extraordinarily short space of six days, reaching here on the afternoon of Tuesday, 21st ult. To our intense disappointment, we missed the *Kroo Boy*, that vessel having, by a conjunction of most unexpected circumstances, left here on Thursday, 16th August—the day after Mr. Henderson's letter reached us at Fìanàrantsòa. No other vessel was at anchor in the roadstead

" On Thursday morning, August 23rd, a large steamer was sighted off here, and we hoisted signals of distress to her, being willing to make any effort whatever to get off, instead of staying here an indefinite period. As we afterwards learned, our signals were observed by her, but they were unnecessary, as she was making for this port, and proved to be H.M.S. *Dryad*, Commander Johnstone.

" Leaving Mrs. Pearse to get ready for embarking, I went on board, and having been invited by Commander Johnstone to his cabin, pleaded with him to take us on board, assuring him that we were willing to put up with any inconvenience, until he could land us at Mauritius, or any other place from which Mrs. Pearse and the children could embark for England. Again we were to be disappointed. Commander Johnstone assured me that he would help me if he could, but said ' I cannot.' He was very reserved about his future, and did not assign any other reason for his ' cannot' than that he did not know the future of his own movements. Before I left the ship, he called me to him a second time, and advising me by all means to remain here, added, ' In a fortnight I may be able to do something for you.' The fortnight expires to-morrow, and we are waiting with intense anxiety for the 'something' to appear."

Commander Johnstone called in H.M.S. *Dryad* on 20th September and took the party over to Mauritius, showing them much care and attention, and earning their warm gratitude.

Mr. Pearse returned to his work, and says of the condition of affairs in Bètsilèo : " This part of Madagascar remains quiet, but our work is somewhat affected by the general unrest and by the continued preparations which the people are making to resist the enemy."

And again: "Our work is in no sense stopped but the excitement, unrest and warlike preparations interfere with that quiet progress forward, which might have been witnessed but for the continuance of war."

Early in 1883 a conference had been held with the Norwegian missionaries, with a view to securing some mutual agreement, and it was eventually decided that each society should acquaint the other before erecting a new church, that certain churches of each society should be closed and that members, church officers, teachers and scholars belonging to the one society should not be accepted by the other without enquiry and arrangement between the missionaries. This latter agreement had become necessary as some, who for reasons of church discipline had been ejected by the one society, might be received by the other, and serious rivalry result.

It was hoped that the result of the conference would have been a considerable improvement in the mutual relations of the two missions. Time, however, proved these hopes to be doomed to disappointment, and the matter was considered to be of such urgency that Mr. Pearse was encouraged by his committee to antedate his furlough by a few months in order to lay the difficulties in person before the directors, and try and obtain through their conference with the directors of the Norwegian Society some *modus vivendi* of a more satisfactory character. On this account, in the month of February, 1885, Mr. Pearse returned to England and terminated his second period of ten years service in Madagascar.

Mr. Pearse joined his family in Edinburgh, which was his headquarters during that furlough. He had, as before, much deputation work to do, but he was able to take advantage of his residence in that city to do a good deal of medical study, and so fit himself further for his medical duties.   Mrs. Pearse's health improved, and thus in May, 1886, they were both of them able to return to Madagascar, without however the joy of any of their family going with them.   The voyage to Mauritius was uneventful but that from that island to Madagascar was far from lacking in interest and this is graphically described in the following chapter.

CHAPTER IX

How we reached Mànanjàra
A Voyage from Port Louis to Madagascar

" LOOSE your sails, for the pilot will be on board in a
few minutes." Such were the instructions which, as
I stood on the deck of the *Sophia*, I heard given to the
chief mate of that vessel, on the morning of Tuesday,
27th July, 1886. Soon after ten o'clock the pilot came
on board, and having completed the preliminary arrangements necessary for starting the vessel, he shouted to
a man who was waiting for the command, " Let go your
hawser," when, with a gentle breeze, the *Sophia* dipped
her flag three times, the seaman's professional way of
saying " good-bye " when starting on a voyage.

The distance from Port Louis to Mànanjàra is about
500 miles, and our thoughts on leaving the harbour were
that perhaps on Friday, but at the latest on Saturday,
we should land at the port for which we were bound.
We were, however, to find that the doings of our little
barque could not be calculated with the accuracy with
which we had been able to forecast the runs of the Castle
Mail Packets *Garth* and *Duart*, in the former of which
we had come from England to Cape Town, and in the
latter, from Cape Town to Mauritius.

During Thursday we were almost becalmed off
Réunion, but once away from that island, the wind
favoured us, and at nine o'clock on Saturday evening, the

captain estimated that we could not be more than about twenty-five miles from the land ; and fearing to approach nearer in the night to a coast which he was now making for the first time, where coral reefs abound, and where there are no lighthouses, he ordered the vessel to be put "about," and for four hours the *Sophia* retraced her course, when she was again "bouted," and her bow put for the land.

The morning of Sunday was cloudy and rainy, and no land could be seen when I went on deck at six o'clock At noon the sun was obscured and no observation could be taken, and it was late in the afternoon before the weather cleared ; even then, however, land was not in sight. On Monday morning it was seen on the distant horizon, and the captain greeted me jocularly, saying, " Here we are, somewhere off the coast of Madagascar." Our hopes were raised, and we confidently assured ourselves that ere the sun set we should be at anchor off Mànanjàra, if not on shore there. Alas ! we were sadly disappointed, for neither that day, nor the next, nor the day after, nor indeed for sixteen days from that morning of bright hopes, did we see the port for which we were bound. A gentle breeze carried us slowly on-ward toward the land, till, at noon, the captain took his observation, when to his surprise and to our intense disappointment he found that his " somewhere " of the morning was seventy-five miles to the south of Mànanjàra !

The order " to the north " was immediately given ; and the wind being favourable, we tried to believe that after all, the mistake would not prove a very serious affair. During Monday afternoon and night we did so well that, " reckoning by the log," we were said, on Tuesday morning, to be only some fifteen miles from

our destination. The day unfortunately proved cloudy
and wet, and for the second time no observation could
be taken at noon ; and although we kept pretty close
to the shore, no Mànanjàra could be descried before
the sun went down. For fear of passing it during the
night, if we continued to go north, the vessel was kept
" on and off " till the morning ; then, however, things
grew worse rather than better, for from early dawn till
evening it rained without intermission, and again no
observation could be taken at noon. No one knew our
actual position, so till twelve o'clock on Thursday, the
Sophia took short trips—now a little way to the north,
and then back to the south, the captain hoping thus
neither to gain nor lose until he could make sure of his
position. On Thursday the weather was fine and
the sky clear, and a good observation was obtained at
noon, when it was found that we were eighty-eight miles
to the south of Mànanjàra, or thirteen miles further
wrong than we were discovered to have been on the
Monday when we first made the land ! The blame was
laid to the current, which the captain had been informed
set to the north, but which he now discovered set strong
to the south.

Again, " to the north " was the order of the day ;
but now the breeze was not so good as when the first
mistake was discovered, and during the next twenty-
four hours we did only thirty-three miles, still leaving
fifty-five between us and Mànanjàra. At this stage of
the voyage we were becalmed for a short time, but the
monotony of the calm was soon relieved by a strong
breeze from the north-east, which effectually prevented
any progress being made in the direction in which we
wished to go. This continued for forty-eight hours,
with the result that on Sunday at noon we were declared

to be 101 miles to the south of Mànanjàra; in addition to
which we had gone away from the land and were again
" somewhere " to the east of Madagascar. During the
Friday night our troubles had nearly reached their
climax, for the darkness concealed the proximity in
which the vessel was at one time to the shore, and the
captain coming to me on Saturday, said: " We were
very close to the reef last night, only about a ship's
length from it ! "

The north-east wind sank into another calm, which
continued till we " turned in " on Sunday night ; but
on Monday morning, it was our joy to find a breeze
from the south filling our sails, and the land again in
sight. The observation at noon, however, showed that
we had not made any progress, but that we were further
to the south than ever. On Tuesday, the north-east
wind again set in, and our latitude at noon was twenty-
four degrees south, another fifty-nine miles being
thus added to our distance from Mànanjàra. We had
now been out fourteen days !

On Wednesday hope revived in our hearts. A strong
south-east breeze had set in during the night, and on
going on deck I found our barque with all sails set and
filled, and that we were running to the north at the rate of
eight knots an hour. With some variation in its strength,
this breeze continued for twenty-four hours, enabling
the captain to say : " I have made my latitude now, at
any rate." Of course this was only a guess " by the
log," but the log does not tell the absolute truth, and the
sun had to be waited for at noon to confirm the estimate,
or to show how much it was wrong. How anxiously
we looked at the heavens as noon drew near ! It had
been cloudy with occasional squalls, since sunrise, and as
twelve o'clock approached, alas ! the clouds thickened,

and once more the captain was unable to " get the sun."
About two o'clock in the afternoon, however, land was
sighted ; and a high hill standing out prominently in the
landscape led to the conclusion that the log had perhaps
given a correct estimate of the distance we had run, as
such a hill stands about ten miles inland to the south-
west of Mànanjàra. Now, unfortunately, the wind,
which had been dying since the morning, gave its last
expiring breath and left us in a dead calm ; the sun set
before any objects could be distinguished on the shore,
and we had to pass another night not really knowing
our position except that we were near to a dangerous
coast and that there were ugly coral reefs ahead, the
spray from the sea breaking on which we had seen as
the sun set behind the mountains far away in the west.

Thursday morning was beautifully bright and clear,
but we were still becalmed. As soon as the captain had
taken his observation and finished his calculations, he
came to me and said : " You were right."   The " right "
referred to an opinion which I had expressed earlier in the
day, that we were still some twenty miles to the south
of Mànanjàra, and which I had formed from the position
of our vessel in relation to the hill that stood out so
prominently as we neared the land on the previous
afternoon. Yes ; we were still twenty-one miles to the
south of Mànanjàra, and becalmed ! Should the wind
rise, from what quarter would it come ? If from the
south, or east or even the west, we could reach our
destination in a few hours, but if from the north, it might
yet be many days. We waited for the first breath of
air, and watched for the first ripple on the ocean. The
breath came, and the ripple appeared, soon followed by
little white-crested waves. The wind had risen, but it
was from the north !

Our only chance of getting up to Mànanjàra was by making a long tack, so, steering close by the wind, away we went till ten o'clock at night, when we were some forty miles out at sea. We then turned, and the head of the *Sophia* once more pointed towards Madagascar. By noon on Saturday (August 14th), we were back within a few miles of the shore, but found that instead of gaining by the task we had lost nineteen miles, being that much further to the south than we were at noon the day before. I asked for an explanation of the ugly fact, and was told that it was the current. I suggested anchoring and waiting till the wind changed, and argued with the captain that there could be no greater risk in doing so on that part of the coast where we found ourselves than off Mànanjàra, since one spot is as much exposed as the other; but my suggestion found no favour in his professional eyes. The vessel was ordered " about," and by four p.m. we were again out of sight of land, with our course as due east as if we had been bound for Mauritius instead of Madagascar.

The aspect of things was getting serious, and whether the provisions would last for the indefinite time which seemed to be before us became a practical question of some moment. It was satisfactory to learn that of ship biscuit and salt beef and pork there was a supply sufficient for three months. Whatever else, therefore, might be before us, we should not die of starvation, and with the appetite sufficiently keen, we might come to relish even hard biscuit and the sailors' " junk." We were already undergoing a training calculated to lead to that issue. The *Sophia* was not a passenger vessel; she had no accommodation for passengers and made but small provision for the wants of those she took from Port Louis. No fresh or tinned meats or any kind

of poultry was laid in, even for those of us who, by
courtesy, were styled " cabin passengers " ; so, even
from the first, the cook did not indulge us with luxuries
or cause us to fare sumptuously. Out of the limited
means at his disposal he provided for us two meals a
day, to the latter of which, served about sunset, he, was
wont to call us by saying : " You take some breakfast ? "
He was a good-hearted Swedish youth, with only an
imperfect knowledge of English. The dish upon which
he most frequently exercised his culinary skill was a
stew of cabbage, onions and potatoes, with just a
flavouring of salt meat, and this generally appeared
at both morning and evening meals. With cabbage
we were supplied in excess from the beginning to the
close of the voyage, leading a fellow-passenger to remark :
" Me eat cabbage morning, me eat cabbage mid-day,
me eat cabbage night, me no want cabbage any more ! "

The breeze which took us away from the land was
succeeded by a calm which lasted forty hours, but
on Monday evening a fair wind sprang up ; and just
as the sun was setting on Tuesday we sighted land
again, but it was still far, far away on the western
horizon. The captain was confident that he was all
right this time ; and although he could hardly expect
to make the port in the night, having no lights on shore
to guide him, he decided to continue his course forward,
and said that he should anchor off whatever part of
the coast he might happen to make, and there wait
till the morning revealed the exact position. Accordingly forward we went with a capital breeze. At eight
o'clock the moon rose in an unclouded sky, and by
nine o'clock it was evident that the land was pretty
near. Soon a light was distinguished, and close observation discovered that it was from a vessel ahead of us.

We went cautiously toward it, in the meantime shortening sail and preparing to cast anchor. The vessel ahead was evidently one riding at anchor, so it was certain that at last we had made some port. Gradually we came to a convenient distance from her, when the order rang out : " Let go the anchor " and the music of the chain running out gladdened our ears. We were at anchor, but where ? We could not be certain. It was about ten o'clock at night, and we were too far out in the open roadstead to distinguish any objects on the shore. We went below and lay down, asking ourselves, " Is it Mànanjàra ? or Mahèla ? or some other port ? " The morning removed all uncertainty. At day-break the captain sent a boat to the *Planter*, the ship we found at anchor ; and a note was brought back in which was written, " This is Mànanjàra."

CHAPTER X

Work among the Bètsilèo
1886 to 1893

HAVING thus at length arrived in Madagascar, Mr. and Mrs. Pearse journeyed up to Fìanàrantsòa, where they were warmly welcomed on September 4th. They soon resumed their former work and heartily entered upon this new term of service.

On December 28th, Mr. Pearse had to announce a catastrophe:—" I am sorry to have to tell you that the church in this town under my care, known as Antrànobirîky, and the mother church of the Sandra district, has been totally destroyed by fire. The fire broke out in a native house early in the afternoon of Thursday, November 11th, and soon spread to other houses near, and from these to the church. There are no means of extinguishing fires here, and the houses being all covered with grass thatch, and being in close proximity to one another, it is usually a serious affair when a fire breaks out. On the present occasion some seventeen houses were either burnt or pulled down to prevent the flames from spreading. The business of building new churches in Fìanàrantsòa would soon have had to come before us, as those already built were getting into a very dilapidated condition. The fire has caused us to take up the matter without further delay."

This added to the work already in hand the super-intendence of the erection of a new church. The interest of the congregation was aroused and focussed on this object and though the building operations were slowly carried out there was much cordiality, unity and enthusiasm on the part of the people.

From two letters written in August and September, 1887, we quote as follows: " God has honoured us by working through us and has given us the joy of knowing that we have been able to do at least a *little* good since our return.

" In November last year, as I informed you in a previous letter, the old church was entirely destroyed by fire, and since that lamentable event, we have held our services in the boys' normal school. The work of building the new church is proceeding, and the pastors and the members of the church and congregation are entering heartily into it. One good man among the natives has given seventy dollars and the manner in which he gave it, and his remarks on the occasion of handing in the amount were as pleasing as the large number of dollars he gave.

" Mr. Sibree has kindly furnished the plans. Building operations are not carried on here with that rapidity with which you are familiar in England, and it will probably be quite twelve months from this date before the new building is ready for opening. We have had great difficulty in getting the large timbers, especially six beams thirty-six feet long by twelve inches by six inches. They have to be cut in the forest very much larger than this, and then dragged here without any mechanical appliance whatever, so that it takes about 150 fellows to bring in one log and then we work them down to the required dimensions.

"Our school in connection with ' Antrànobirìky ' is only a preparatory one, and as soon as the children have mastered the three ' Rs,' or a little more, they are drafted off to the higher schools under the care of our friends Mr. Huckett and Miss Frédoux. Mrs. Pearse is able to take an interest in the girls connected with this latter school. She also finds much pleasure in conducting a weekly Bible class for the women and in visiting one of our near country stations, that of Ankàranòsy, once a fortnight. In conjunction with Mrs. Johnson, she holds a meeting for women in our house every Tuesday. The women are very much attached to her, and by God's blessing, she is doing a good work among them. She has the great grace of being ' patient to all.'

"The medical mission takes up much of my time, but both the directors and the district committee here have recognised that as my *special* work, and through it we are undoubtedly doing much to further the highest interests of the mission, while in itself it is a great blessing to many sufferers. Throughout the year there have been a total of some two thousand different cases brought to us, which, giving to each an average of five attendances, makes ten thousand attendances in the year. The medicines are still supplied gratis, but voluntary contributions are solicited from the patients. Many, especially the Bètsilèo, give nothing, but the amount given by the Hovas is sometimes satisfactory. I have had 12s., 10s., 8s., and so on, from individual patients. The total amount of voluntary contributions for the year, and the sale of a few medicines, is about £20. The ' cases ' have been very various ; we have had six cases of hare-lip to operate on, also a very severe accident, whereby the lower jaw was broken in six pieces and the flesh dreadfully lacerated and burnt.

"The district under my care is *not* in a flourishing condition, with the exception of one portion of it. This portion, which consists of a group of ten churches and schools gives me great satisfaction and joy. God is working, and, without doubt, His kingdom is advancing there. All the work is in a flourishing condition, for which we thank God and take courage. The evangelist is an exceptionally good one, and his personal character such that he exercises a great influence for good in this portion of my district, of which he has the charge.

"The western portion of the district is in a *most un-satisfactory* condition, and with the limited time at my disposal for working it, and the great difficulties connected with it, I sometimes almost despair of making anything of it. It has a bad history; the native evangelists who have worked in it have not turned out well; and, during the past year, the population has been kept in a state of constant unrest and terror, on account of the frequent attacks made upon them by bands of robbers from the west. These have destroyed and burnt many villages; stolen large numbers of cattle; killed many young men, and carried many women and children away into slavery."

In his letter he emphasizes again the difficulties of overlapping, due to the presence of two missions on the same ground, and he says, " I will reiterate my deep conviction that both the Protestant societies cannot be successful, and repeat my opinion that time, strength, influence and funds are being unwisely expended. The matter has caused, and still causes me constant anxiety and sorrow, and is affecting my health not a little. "Can nothing yet be done? Is it beyond what is practical for a deputation to come out here to take an

unprejudiced view of the relative positions ? Can
nothing be suggested, or no arrangement made between
the two societies, by which God may be more glorified
than at present, and the still heathen parts of Madagascar
reached, instead of Protestant missionaries being in one
another's way, as it is at present in this part of the island ?
Serious mistakes have been made in the past, but when
they are discovered, it is surely better that they should
be remedied (if possible), than that they should be
continued."

It was not until Christmas, 1889, that the new church
was ready for the opening ceremonies. During that
year Mr. and Mrs. Pearse had had the joy of welcoming
one of their daughters, who came out in order to keep
house for her father, and so release Mrs. Pearse to return
to her family in Edinburgh.

The church-opening was described by Mr. Pearse in
a paper to the *Chronicle*, from which the following
extracts are made :—

" Christmas week was a season of unusual interest
and of no little excitement with us in Fìanàrantsòa, for
on Christmas day, and the two following days we held
services in connection with the opening of Antrànobirìky
new church. The fire which destroyed the old church was
looked upon as a great calamity at the time, but, as has
since been said over and over again by the natives, the
calamity has turned out to be a blessing. The new
church is a great improvement on the old one, and its
erection has called forth the earnestness of the people,
and developed their liberality. The church has been
nearly three years in erection. We have been long about
it, but, in every respect, I think the work is well done,
and without an earthquake should give the building a
rough shake, or it should be unfortunate enough to be

struck by lightning, the building will serve as a house of prayer for several generations to come.

"We are indebted to the Rev. J. Sibree for all the plans from which the building has been erected. Our dear friend expended much time and trouble upon them and the congregation owe him a debt of great gratitude.

"In Madagascar Christmas comes after the wet season has commenced, and when the congregation decided to hold the opening services at Christmas, some of us had fears that the weather would interfere with the success of the engagements. However, like many other fears, we found that we need not have entertained them, for on the morning of Christmas day the sky was unclouded, and with the exception of a few slight showers on Friday, the 27th December, the weather continued fine till the services were over. One of our good native friends recognized this as evidence that God was smiling upon our undertaking, and in his prayer he said : 'Thou hast kept back the hail ; Thou hast restrained the wind ; Thou hast withheld the lightning ; and Thou hast also bid the rain wait for a season, that we might hold these services.'

"At eight o'clock the first service commenced with singing. At the close of the hymn I read a few short passages from the Bible, and the elder of the two native pastors offered thanksgiving for the successful completion of the building. Then followed a little business, purely native in its character. The congregation had written to inform Her Majesty the Queen of Madagascar, and the Prime Minister, also the church in Antanànarìvo, of which they are members, of the completion and proposed opening of the new church, and, to show their interest in the work and to express their Christian sympathy, Ràinimànga, one of the influential pastors in the city was sent down to represent them on the occasion of the opening. He brought with him a letter from the Queen and Prime Minister. This letter was read to the congregation, after which Ràinimànga made a short speech, in which he said that Her Majesty the Queen, and the Prime Minister, and their church, were pleased to learn what the people in the south had done, and that he had been sent to represent them on the occasion of opening the church. He added that they had not sent him empty-handed, but that to give a practical expression of their sympathy, they had sent by him a donation of fifty dollars (£10) towards the building fund. This gave great delight to the people. Then, as is customary on all public occasions in this country, the people, through a representative of high rank, presented a dollar as a token of their unbroken allegiance to Her Majesty, Rànavàlona III., and the speaker expressed the gratitude of the people for the sympathy shown by the Queen in sending Ràinimànga, and their delight that he had brought such a handsome donation. All this was done " decently and in order." Later on Ràrinòsy, the second pastor, read a paper giving a brief history of the church, from which it appeared that it is only about thirty years since, in the midst of persecution, Christianity was introduced to the town of Fìanàrantsòa. An excellent sermon was preached by our brother, Rev. A. S. Huckett.

" The afternoon service was fixed for one o'clock, but before that hour the building was again crowded. At this service a financial statement was read, from which it appeared that the total amount expended on the church had been a little under two thousand dollars (£400). The sum of £100 was granted us by the London Missionary Society, over £120 was raised by the

natives, and the remainder was given by various
friends, as Erskine Beveridge, Esq., and my kind friend
Mr. Card, of Lewes.

"Altogether the services have been a great success.
There is much darkness still in some parts of Madagascar,
but the light is increasing. Christianity is extending
its roots and spreading its branches and it is becoming a
greater power in the island."

Mr. Pearse was seldom free from building responsibilities; when the church was opened he proceeded
with the erection of a more commodious hospital and
dispensary, and he had other important churches to
put up in his district.

In May, 1890, he writes : " I regret to say that a *very*
severe epidemic of remittent fever is raging in the
district, and I am overwrought with work among the
sick." And later : " For the past few years the west
and north-west districts have been greatly disturbed on
account of raids made by bands of robbers and others,
who only nominally acknowledge the Hova authority.
Much distress has been caused among the people and
the work in some of our churches and schools has been
greatly interrupted. These lawless bands have of late
been getting bolder and bolder, and only within the
past month attacked the immediate neighbourhood of
a mission station, burning the native dwellings, destroying property, stealing cattle, and carrying off women
and children. This has caused quite a panic, and many
of the inhabitants have fled.

"Really you must see if the London Missionary
Society, or some other society, cannot send a doctor
to take on the medical work here. I have never
cried out about work, but I do not think I can
stand it much longer. This year, 1890, has been

one unparalleled in my experience for sickness among the natives.

" The simple truth is that with only two of us here to attend to the work in its various departments (Mr. Huckett was in England on furlough), we sometimes have not leisure to take our meals properly. Thank God, myself and Mr. Johnson are strong young men (?) and we have both a sort of natural liking for hard work, and so what does it matter, so be that by all we do we are glorifying the Master, extending His kingdom and doing good to those among whom He has sent us to live and labour."

A year after the opening of the church, the hospital was finished, and an interesting ceremony of dedication was held on December 26th, 1891. Mr. Johnson, after praising the site, describes the building, which has on the ground floor a large waiting-room, consultation and dispensing rooms ; in the upper storey one large ward and two private wards ; there were also detached cottages suitable for other patients. The building was well named " Ambàlamàhatsàra " (the place to get better).

It was Mr. Pearse's custom to hold a brief service in the waiting-room, where was collected a motley crowd, dressed in differing styles, from the clean white lamba and pretty print dress of the Hova, to the coarse mat in which some poor Bètsilèo would be attired, giving to them the appearance, as they sat on the floor, of a head and feet emerging at either end of a roll of matting. Numbered tickets were served out to the patients in their order of arrival, and on the handbell receiving a smart tap, the sick would be ushered one by one into the presence of their physician. Then a few questions would elicit their symptoms or their progress, if it

happened to be an old patient ; further details needing
examination were attended to in a side room, but if
they were not necessary, during the conversation, which
was very strictly but kindly kept to the point, the
bottle would be filled by Mr. Pearse's own hand with the
medicine prescribed, and without any loss of time,
but with a word of cheer, the visit would terminate and
the next patient be shown in.   If dentistry happened
to be the sad necessity, with the most marvellous skill
and rapidity the extraction was performed.   In this
way, beginning early about 7.30 and going on till 12, a
total of about a hundred patients would be seen, sometimes rather fewer, sometimes many more.

Those needing retention in hospital were taken in,
and an occasional operation was performed, for the
relief of such things as stone, hare-lip, and tumours, as
well as for emergency cases that now and again presented
themselves, such as bullet wounds, cuts and stabs from
the attacks of robber bandits.   The native custom of
bringing a large retinue of friends lent itself to the increase
of the influence of the medical missionary, as a few words
addressed to the patient or one of the friends were
received by a very much larger audience and discussed.
Mr. Pearse says: "Just now I have a child about four
years of age and his father, grandmother and sister
occupying one of the rooms of our house.   The little
fellow was operated on and is doing well."

In another letter he describes a sad case illustrating
in a flagrant manner the customs of the Bètsilèo in their
treatment of the sick.   "Yesterday," he says, "I had
an urgent request that I would go and see a sick woman
some little distance away from here.   On arriving at the
place, I found a young woman in a dying condition,
in a miserable, dark and dirty hut, and quite beyond any

FIANÀRANTSÒA.—MR. PEARSE'S CHURCH ON SUMMIT.

assistance that I could render. She had been seriously ill for ten days, I asked the family what they had done for her. 'Oh,' they said, 'we have had two of our native medicine men and they told us to kill a fowl and all to eat of it, and they also told us to get native-made rum and all to drink of it, and,' they continued, 'we have done this, but the young woman is no better.' Had my knowledge and skill been sought a week before, she might have lived. Many of our poor folk fall victims to their superstitions and to the ignorance and wicked folly of the medicine men among them."

Other features of the medical work are brought out by Rajaònimarîa in his recollections.

In the *Chronicle* for August, 1891, Mr. Pearse picturesquely describes another church opening. He says: " For several years past, the people in connection with the town of Fànjakàna have been engaged in building a new chapel and it had been arranged to hold the opening services on Friday, May 1st. Accompanied by Miss Frédoux and my daughter, I arrived there on the previous Tuesday evening and spent the Wednesday and part of Thursday in conducting the annual examination of the children from all the schools in the district. Much to the satisfaction of all, the morning of Friday was fine, and, so far as the weather was concerned, we had a magnificent day—much such a day as the brightest of May days in England.

" The new chapel is a fairly good specimen of the present day village chapel in Bètsilèo. The walls are thoroughly substantial, being four bricks thick. The inside is neatly finished off, and the accommodation is sufficient for about a thousand people. On ordinary occasions the chapel is not likely to be full until indeed the showers of blessing, for which we long, come

down upon the Bètsilèo, and they manifest a willingness
to seek the Lord which they do not show at present.

" On the day of opening, the building was filled by a
congregation which was of a most mixed description·
There were several evangelists there—young Malagasy,
who have had considerable missionary influence brought
to bear upon them, who have been educated in the
London Missionary Society's College at Antanànarîvo,
and who may be spoken of as the most advanced among
the Malagasy, in intelligence and general knowledge.
There were not a few of the rising generation of Hovas—
youths who have had a good education in some of our
schools, who have a great liking for boots and fancy
stockings and other articles of European attire,whose vote
is decidedly in favour of Christianity, but whose general
condition often causes the missionary grave anxiety.
There were also a limited number of Hova ladies
dressed in their best—some in light blue and bright
yellow and pink silk ' lambas,' while one wore a skirt
said to be of ' grass green silk, trimmed with satin
frills of crimson, orange and grey, at the side was a
purple rosette with a big button in the middle.'

" And then, lastly, there were very many of the poor
Bètsilèo—some with the charms, of which they think
so much, on their neck, feet and wrist, or tied in their
hair, and one here and another there with only a small
rush mat for clothing. As I sat looking at these, their
gross ignorance and intense spiritual darkness made me
inwardly sigh and weep. For once again the poor and
the rich met together, and the comparatively enlightened
and the utterly ignorant were gathered within the same
building. Outwardly there was much difference in
the appearance of the people who made up the vast
congregation, but it may be that not so much inward

difference was visible to Him, who looks not at the outward appearance but at the hearts of all.

"Upon the whole, we were glad and thankful for what we saw and heard that day at Fànjakàna. I have often been heavy at heart about the Lord's work there ; the soil seems peculiarly unfavourable to the growth of the gospel. It is over twenty years since the gospel was first introduced there ; the Rev. C. T. Price lived and laboured faithfully there for several years ; other missionaries and native workers have visited and worked there, but notwithstanding all that has been done, the inhabitants in whom I have confidence that they are really born again, and are new creatures in Christ Jesus, are few indeed. The time to favour Fànjakàna will yet come ; this must be our hope, and for this we pray."

In the month of March, 1892, Mr. Pearse writes of a very different experience : " I regret to have to inform you that three weeks ago, the whole of Bètsilèo was visited by a severe hurricane of wind and rain. A hurricane of such force and continuance is not remembered by the oldest inhabitant, with whom I have conversed. Many of our chapels in the country have been unroofed and otherwise seriously damaged. The house which I have occupied since 1881 had the whole of the north verandah and balcony swept away, and the building is now in such a dilapidated condition that there is no course open for us than to proceed immediately with repairs."

In the month of March, 1893, the mission was called upon to suffer the loss of Rev. R. Roberts, their youngest member. The circumstances of his unexpected death were very sad, especially so as he was living at a day's journey from Fìanàrantsòa and Mr. Pearse was actually

not in possession of the letter summoning his attendance
until four hours after the fatal event had supervened.
Such crises in the domestic experience of missionary
families are extremely distressing, and there is always
the poignant feeling of regret, when distance makes
it impossible to arrive in time to give the necessary aid.
In these days of greater speed-advantages it is to be
hoped that such events will be of even much greater
rarity than in the past. Mr. Roberts had attained a
good working knowledge of the language and was regarded as an excellent worker of very promising character. At the time of this sad death, Mr. Pearse was
contemplating returning to England on furlough, and
had formed the desire of visiting Antanànarìvo and
Antsihànaka, with a view of noting the progress of the
gospel in the places where he had formerly laboured.
It was, however, necessary to alter these plans, in order
that the widowed Mrs. Roberts might have the benefit
of the help of Mr. Pearse and his daughter in the difficulties of the voyage.   They left in the month of June,
1893, and travelling via the Cape of Good Hope arrived
in England in August. As before, the family headquarters were at Edinburgh, where a joyful reunion took
place.

A pretty little incident has come to light in connection
with this furlough. When in Edinburgh, Mr. Pearse
was in the habit of taking his youngest daughter to her
school at George Watson's College every day.   Noticing
the numbers of young girls who flocked there, he was led
to think of their welfare and he had a little card printed
with the following words :

" God is Love.

" God loves *you*.

" God wants you to be happy—to be very, very happy.

Happy every day. Happy all the day. Happy at home from morning till evening. Happy at school from the time you go in till the time you come away. Happy during the holidays from the first day till the last. Yes; happy always, and happy everywhere.

"School-days are the spring-time of life, and the flower of joy should flourish in every young heart.

"I hope that you are thus happy."

When this was ready, he asked the Headmaster's permission to say a few words to the girls, and each one was given one of the cards.

At this time also he undertook the task of collecting a donation to be presented at the Centenary of the London Missionary Society, as a contribution from its missionaries. More than £100 was received, but he was deprived of the pleasure of making the presentation as he had by that time returned to Madagascar.

CHAPTER XI

Troublous Times

1894 to 1896

Towards the close of 1894 the intention of the French government to send a Plenipotentiary to the court of Madagascar, prepared if necessary to present an ultimatum embodying its demands, became known. On hearing of this, Mr. Pearse wrote to the Rev. R. Wardlaw Thompson to the following effect, under the date 15th September, 1894 : " We have noticed in the *Times* of last week that there is reason to fear that, after a few months, war may again break out between France and Madagascar. This has led Mrs. Pearse and myself, and the members of our family, who are at home, very carefully to consider our position in relation to our future work, and to the people among whom we have lived and laboured so long, and to whom we are bound by very close and affectionate ties. The result is that we have decided that it is my duty to return to Madagascar *at once*, so that I may be among the people, should new troubles indeed come upon them, and that I may avoid the risk of not being able to get into the country if my return is delayed until the spring. I therefore write to tell you that I am willing and ready to go (D.V.) by the first vessel in which you can take passage for me." The feeling of the board on the subject was that it was premature to take action on the political possibilities, and that the renewal of his vigour by a more prolonged furlough was of greater immediate importance, both to Mr. Pearse personally and to the interests of the work.

The matter, however, was not allowed to rest, and after the rupture of relations between France and Madagascar in the month of November, a fresh offer on Mr. Pearse's part was acceded to by the board. Consequently on the 8th February, 1895, he started in the *Roslin Castle*, this time alone, for his fourth term of service. There was an entire lack of incident during the voyage, but the entries in the diaries of this period show that there were three leading thoughts in Mr. Pearse's mind: the hard lot that came to him in his entire separation from all his family; his consciousness of Divine guidance and realization of Divine help in his need; and, as the voyage proceeded, an ever-increasing anxiety as to his prospects of being able to land in Madagascar, after the declaration of war.

He says: "I was reading in Matthew after breakfast, and there heard the Master saying : ' Be of good cheer.' I was much struck too with the way in which He anticipated his sufferings and death. *He* did not think it strange concerning the fiery trial which He was to pass through. May I be filled with His Spirit, then I shall not think the cross I am carrying too heavy to bear. But it is *not* a light thing to be separated from you all, my children, and yet how little, how very little, have I had these, who are really mine, about me.

" About a dozen of us joined in singing a few familiar hymns. It was delightful and about the happiest half-hour I have spent on board.

> "Since thy Father's arm sustains thee
> Peaceful be! peaceful be!"

He transhipped at Durban, found a fellow-passenger in Mr. E. F. Knight, the well-known author, who was going to Madagascar as war correspondent for the *Times*, and on Sunday, 17th March, their vessel touched at Fort Dauphin, the most southerly port in Madagascar. The pros and cons of landing there, and journeying by land to Fìanàrantsòa, as against running the risk of blockade or stormy weather at Mànanjàra, the usual port, were exhaustively discussed, and when they found themselves off the coast of Madagascar and able to land, they decided to go on shore then and there.

Mr. Knight says : "A fellow passenger on the *Dunbar Castle*, whose destination was Fìanàrantsòa, and who had come to the same decision as myself, disembarked with me. This was the Rev. J. Pearse, of the London Missionary Society, a gentleman whose knowledge of the Malagasy language and of the inhabitants is probably second to that of no other white man in the island. He was my companion for the first and most difficult half of my long journey. In this I was very fortunate. He was a capital fellow-traveller, and his long experience of native ways extricated us without loss of dignity from many a trouble with aggressive savages." " We had the greatest difficulty in procuring bearers ; for three days we sought men in vain ; all were afraid to accompany us through the disturbed districts, but, happily for us, a Norwegian missionary, Mr. Nilsen, happened to arrive at Fort Dauphin with a considerable following of men, Bètsilèo and Tanala, who were anxious to return to their homes, and were therefore glad to accompany us. These men, however, knowing that it was impossible for us to engage others, insisted on an exorbitant rate of pay. As a rule, the Malagasy bearers are cheery, willing fellows, but these particular men were lazy and

mutinous, far more troublesome rascals, Mr. Pearse
assured me, than he ever before had dealings with, in
all his thirty years experience in the country. We set
out on our journey on March 20th. It was our intention
to follow the coast as far as Vàngaïndràno, the next
Hova military post, a distance of 150 miles, and thence
to strike across the Tanala country to the Bètsilèo
highlands. Six men lightly loaded carried our baggage
and stores, and we engaged eight palanquin bearers
each. These trained bearers, relieving each other at
frequent intervals, can carry a man thirty miles a
day, if the conditions .are favourable ; but on this
journey we averaged about twenty miles a day, for our
progress was necessarily slow across the deep swamps.
The numerous difficult fords, and the broad rivers which
had to be crossed in small, dug-out canoes, caused much
delay, while the forest paths were generally too narrow
to allow of two men going abreast, so that we had to
walk no inconsiderable portion of the distance."

Mr. Pearse summarizes the experiences of these weeks
in a very few words ; he says : " The journey from Fort
Dauphin occupied me twenty days, and was very
difficult and trying. As all my luggage was left on the
steamer, I had not many comforts or luxuries, and in
honest truth I had to rough it considerably. By night
I spread my rug on the mud floor of the native hut
and rested my head on a borrowed pillow, but I generally
slept, being tired with the day's journey. I was thoroughly worn out when I arrived, and quite broken down
with the heavy strain that had been upon me. God was
very good in granting me fine weather during the greater
part of the land journey. Since my arrival I have had
four attacks of fever."

He adds : " I have had a *very* kind reception from

my missionary brethren and sisters, and also from all classes of the natives. I have had numerous visitors, and am over-stocked with live poultry. Altogether I must have received over thirty turkeys. I have distributed them at the hospital and among the students, and have sent some to my friends. Only yesterday a woman came and her eyes were full of tears, as she tried to tell me how glad she was that I had come back. I am going to occupy two rooms in our own house, but I shall probably have my principal meals with Mr. and Mrs. Johnson. I do not find that many changes have taken place. The thing that strikes me is the absence of the Roman Catholic priests and sisters, all of whom left six months ago.

"My church has been well cared for, and the building looks neat and clean, and even bears favourable comparison with many of the buildings in which I conducted services at home. I fancy that it is much better than some of you imagine, and that you would be not a little surprised if you could look at it. The hospital, cottages and grounds connected therewith have also been well cared for, and give me much satisfaction as I look on them. The work in the hospital has developed in the hands of Dr. Peake and there are more in-patients than when the medical mission was in my hands. The doctor has been away, and so my services have been in pretty frequent demand."

Mr. Pearse soon found himself busily engaged in his usual duties. He thus refers to his personal habits: "I rise about 5.30 a.m. and get tea brought me by six. At seven I am called to breakfast. We dine at twelve, take tea at five, after which I come back to my rooms, and about nine the man brings me a little cornflour for my supper. I am often asleep by ten."

One of the earliest demands on his medical skill was in answer to a call to nurse Rev. Thomas Brockway, who was exceedingly ill with malaria, a day's journey from Fìanàrantsòa. His tactful care was ultimately rewarded with success.

Mr. Pearse thus embarked upon what proved to be by far the most trying and difficult of his terms of service. Difficulties had not been wanting before, but they were such as he could hope to vanquish by his courage and his industry, his exceedingly orderly habit of mind enabling him to overtake a routine of work, astonishing in its variety and amount. This time the routine was to be rudely broken, and he was called upon, with his brethren, to suffer persecution, disappointment, enmity, and bitterness, sufficient to have crushed less faithful and valorous souls.

During 1895, however, there was very little sign of the coming storm. Work went on as usual. His preaching and Bible-classes in town and in the district, his dispensing in the country and also at times, during Dr. Peake's absence, in Fìanàrantsòa, and his writing, all proceeded with regularity, broken only by attacks of malaria, which frequently laid him low. Even within a fortnight of the bombardment of Antanànarìvo he was able to record in his diary the holding of exceedingly successful meetings in connection with the native missionary society. He says of one meeting : " Found the church overcrowded. Rum and slavery—some very plain words were spoken about these, and it is interesting to observe how decidedly public opinion is rising against them. Very plain and earnest addresses on ' unjust and unchristian dealings with others.' Cheating, lying, usury, and various kinds of oppression were spoken about in no uncertain language. I was surprised at the boldness of the speaker, and at the universal acceptance by the meeting of his denunciations."

After the news of the capitulation, on September 30th, 1895, had reached Fìanàrantsòa, it was the duty and privilege of the missionaries to try and allay the fears natural to such an occasion. There are such entries as this : " I tried to strengthen and cheer the poor folk. It is a great comfort to them that we are here. But for our presence there would have been quite a panic from fear." " I called all the pastors and evangelists to meet me, and we had a capital gathering. I tried to allay their anxieties and fears and counselled them as to their conduct and action and work at the present crisis." There were wild rumours afloat, that all the men would be killed and all the women and children deported. Also that only those connected with the Roman Catholics would be safe. Still, in spite of the crisis they had passed through, things seemed to speedily settle down again ; one sign of this was the resumption of ordinary work, as he is soon able to write in his diary : " I am getting on with my commentary on 2 Corinthians."

In November, there were a few indications of trouble, for he writes : " I received a long letter from an evangelist telling me that the Mompera (Mon père) at Nataò was giving them trouble and causing some of his people to fear with his threats and high-sounding words, and I deemed it advisable to go at once and give all the encouragement I could to the people." And again : " The priests are causing a good deal of commotion in the country and are trying to carry things with a high hand. There are serious troubles before us, I fear, in that quarter." " The Roman Catholics speak of our churches as churches of the devil. In one district the priest bound three men connected with one of our churches and made them pay ten dollars each before releasing them."

In January, he writes: " Nothing out of the ordinary has taken place for some days. I have been engaged pretty constantly on the commentary, and the first part of the manuscript will go to the printer next week. A man came with a dislocated jaw. The doctor was away, so I told him to sit down, and in a minute, to the great astonishment of himself and the Bètsilèo who accompanied him, I put him all right again and sent him home rejoicing."

Early in February, he notes: " I have been dwelling much in thought on the events of this time last year. The corresponding days were my last in England before leaving to return here. It *was* a heavy and trying week, but, as I look back upon it, I can see very clearly how tenderly and lovingly grace was given to us all as the days and hours needed it."

On February 11th, he says: " The resident came into the town officially about mid-day. The priests went out in strong force to meet him and came back to town in procession with him. This was evidently a move on their part to make the impression on the natives that their church is France."

The next day the missionaries officially asked for an interview in order to offer their congratulations and welcome, and then the unexpected blow descended. The interview was at first refused and serious charges were brought against the missionaries, which were verbally repeated when, on the following day, the request for an interview was granted. Concerning this, Mr. Pearse writes: " I was singled out as the specially guilty individual. The accusations brought against us

were immediately and absolutely denied, and we appealed
to the righteousness of the French Republic for the fullest
investigation and trial, the resident having stated in
writing that his ' convictions were not based on a single
fact, but on a collection of concordant facts, precise
and undeniable.' Our appeal met with no response
whatever."

The resident from this time forth showed very
marked favour to the Jesuits as against the London
Missionary Society. In the month of August of the
same year, he responded to a letter from Mr. Pearse,
urgently requesting an opportunity to clear his character,
and he then went the length of offering his hand and
recalling his correspondence, which he tore up in token
of his recognition of the falsehood of the charges.
But in spite of this he was able in one way and another
to place serious difficulties in the way of the cause
of our missionaries. This incident was naturally a
very painful and even dangerous one, and Mr. Pearse
never ceased to regret that the demand for a full
and open investigation of the charges was not acceded
to.

A few days after the resident's arrival, a *kabàry* was
held, that is, a general assemblage of the populace. In
the course of his speech on that occasion he told the
people, amongst other things, that they had liberty to
send their children to whatever school they pleased,
that it was quite optional to them to worship on the
Sundays or not, that there were no restrictions to their
working on that day if they wished and also that they
might rest easy in their minds on the subject of slavery,
because France would not interfere with that. About
this, Mr. Pearse remarks: " The *kabàry* has caused me
more sorrow than any I remember to have attended.

There is much to make us sad, but it will drive us to God, and lead us more than ever to take the work to Him."

There was not much change to record in the character of the work done, and very large gatherings were occasionally noted in the diary. In the month of April, Mr. Pearse spent ten days visiting his district, and his varied experiences were embodied in a paper, which gives so vivid a picture of his life that we quote it somewhat freely.

" Soon after nine o'clock I reached Nasàndratròny, where I visit fortnightly for the purpose of attending to the sick, holding a Bible class, and meeting with teachers, pastors and evangelists from other parts of the district. Some seventy patients claimed my attention and kept me fully occupied till sunset. Sixty of these paid a fee of twopence each for advice and medicine, so that ten shillings stand to the credit of the medical mission to meet the expenses of the day's work. The majority of the cases were sufferers from the fearful epidemic of remittent fever, which is at present raging, and to which a large number have fallen victims. One patient was suffering from the effects of gunshot wounds, received when a band of marauders attacked the homestead where she was living.

" At Nasàndratròny we have one of our neatest chapels and one of our best and most trustworthy evangelists. In the earlier and happier days of mission work in Bètsilèo, the chapel was the only one for the sub-district of which it is the centre. Now there are nine chapels connected with the Norwegian mission and six with the Roman Catholics, a condition involving a most unwise and unnecessary expenditure of time, strength and Christian funds, and producing difficulties and rivalry, and party spirit, which ought to be unknown in the foreign mission field.

" The Bible-class was held unusually early the next morning, and before ten o'clock I was *en route* for my next centre. Alas ! I had not proceeded far before I had unmistakable signs that the fever was attacking with severity the doctor of yesterday. After a very wearisome journey, we arrived soon after five o'clock at a little place consisting of about a dozen huts, surrounded by a thick hedge of prickly pear and with a double gateway built of rough stones and timber. In the centre of this group of huts is a deserted cattle-pen filled with stagnant water. The hut into which I was respectfully invited was a wretched place. Here, in the company of mosquitoes and numerous other insects, I spent an uncomfortable night, with high fever upon me. Next morning we were on the move by seven a.m., and passed through country which has been desolated by banditti. Three places at which the London Missionary Society used to have small village stations are now overgrown with long grass and the tops of a few bare walls showing above it mark where the native huts once stood. It was a very hot day, and by twelve o'clock I felt almost unable to proceed. I bade my bearers put me down by a stream and while they boiled a little water in gipsy fashion, wherewith to make me a cup of tea, I laid myself under the shelter of a bush, with feelings expressed by Jonah in the words ' It is better for me to die than to live.' However, the tea did something for me, and rousing myself, we resumed our journey. About two o'clock we came in sight of Kàlamavòny, and a short distance away from the town we found the school children drawn up to meet me. When the day broke I felt justified by the fall in my temperature in getting ready for the services of the day, and for the pleasurable duty of introducing a new young evangelist and his wife. About nine o'clock I went to the chapel, within which a congregation of probably 800 were crowded, but alas! I had hardly commenced, before I was compelled by the return of the fever to beat an ignominious retreat and take to my stretcher again, where I spent the remainder of that Easter Sunday.

"It has always been a pleasure to me to visit this place. There is a small nucleus of Christians; there are a good many young people in the town, who have passed through our school, and the great majority of the adult population retain their unsophisticated simplicity, knowing nothing of rivalry connected with the 'praying' or of the temptations sometimes held out by proselytizers.

"My condition was beginning to assume a serious aspect, so during Sunday night, I determined to get back to Fìanàrantsòa without delay. Next day, therefore, I started for Fànjakàna, the next station where we have an evangelist, which is within a day's journey of home. What long miles were those twenty-five, over which the men bore me! The country, too, through which we passed was in mourning, for in what was ten years ago a fairly populous district, where large herds of cattle grazed and where we had a congregation and school, there is now not a single inhabitant nor did I see one head of cattle, so complete has been the desolation caused by the robbers. By four o'clock we reached higher ground, and the gentle breeze refreshed me, and the fever began to take its departure. The next morning I was well enough to hold a meeting of the congregation. They were in trouble, some of the

heavier timbers in the roof of their large chapel having
given way, necessitating the rebuilding of the place.
There was very little enthusiasm and the response to my
appeal was extremely feeble. This has ever proved a
stony place, and the visible fruit is, alas! only a few
grains. Both the Norwegians and the Roman Catholics
have come since we built our church, and so, in this
town and in the midst of these ignorant Bètsilèo, there
is the miserable spectacle of three churches.

" While there, one of my bearers hurriedly entered
my apartment, and pointing to his leg from which the
blood was running freely, said that an old ladder had
given way beneath him, with the unwelcome result to
which he directed my attention. It was a matter of a
few minutes to put in a stitch or two and the man was
so little affected that he was able to follow me to the
next place, a distance of about twelve miles.

" ' Accidents never come singly,' for on my arrival at
Alàrobà, the evangelist's wife told me that he had been
walking in his sleep and had fallen from a height of some
twelve feet and sustained a severe shaking and a sprained
ankle. This man has not had any college training,
but the spiritual training which he has experienced
has made him a useful companion in service, and he is
by no means an inefficient worker and preacher of the
gospel. Early next morning I saw several patients and
then started for the next village station. To reach this
place we had to cross a swift, deep and broad river,
and we expected to find the necessary canoe at the
crossing. On arriving, however, no canoe was to be
seen. After about a quarter of an hour my men found
one up the stream, but there were no paddles. There
are, however, ways of working paddleless canoes, for
one man, now by strokes with a couple of sticks, and

now by kicks made alternately with his legs, and anon by wildly splashing with his arms, managed in due time to land us safely on the other side. Our visit to the village was uninspiring, for the chapel was unfinished, the adults indifferent, the teacher lazy and the children uninterested in their lessons and not making progress. There are cloudy days as well as sunny ones in the missionary's calendar, and this was one of the former for me.

" Between this village and the next, we had again to cross the river at a place lower down. Once more there was no canoe, but again the men were fortunate in finding one not far off, again without paddles. In this one, however, there was a hole below the water-line through which the water flowed much too freely to make one willing to attempt a crossing in the primitive manner related above. We therefore used clay in a most scientific and satisfactory manner to plug the opening and were soon landed safe and dry on the opposite shore !

" The next day it was necessary once more to cross the river, but as there is always a government canoe at the crossing, I did not anticipate any difficulties. However, on arriving at the place, I was astonished to find a number of people on either bank, all with their eyes directed towards a small island in the middle of the river, where it appeared that the canoe, improperly moored the previous evening, had drifted during the night. Here there was no second canoe in reserve, and no one had been found willing to risk swimming out to the island, for fear of the crocodiles. But in time two bold fellows made a dash of it through the water and brought the canoe to the bank, and we were soon able to cross.

" At the village we next visited we found 72 scholars gathered together out of 104 written on the register, and I held a Bible class with them, after which, the pastor, who is one of the very few genuine, sincere, simple-minded Bètsilèo, entertained me to a simple meal.

" On the Saturday, after holding a thanksgiving service with the family of the evangelist for his recent merciful preservation from death, I visited two more villages, at one of which I spent the night. After conducting service there on Sunday morning, I returned to Fîanàrantsòa, glad and grateful to reach home in safety and comparative health."

The fever to which allusion has been made was a terrible visitation, and it raged in the district round Fîanàrantsòa from March till June. In the absence of the doctor, Mr. Pearse was again in charge of the medical mission, and his diary records many wearisome days. " Yesterday and to-day I have had over 200 out-patients. To-night I am quite worn out." " An American made a rapid and good recovery, and said this evening ' I never saw fever cured so quickly in my life.' " " The medical work now absorbs nearly all my time and wears me out." He speaks of the epidemic as being of " unprecedented severity, and alarmingly fatal, especially among those natives who despised, or were unable to obtain, European drugs. In one valley alone the natives estimate that there were a thousand deaths. This epidemic cast a gloom over everything. Schools were broken up and churches deserted. Every home had its sick. Every day there were funerals—in some instances women had to open the graves and superintend the burials. Every family was in mourning. From every direction came sounds of wailing. In some of the Bètsilèo homesteads every member of the family died, some under most heart-rending conditions. In one village all had either died or left, except a man and his wife. They were stricken down, and somehow, during their illness got parted, and died in separate huts. During this painful time the value of European drugs and treatment was recognized by a great number of the natives, and the applications to us for medicines were many, urgent and pathetic; indeed, the demand was so great that the supply failed, and for a few days, to our deep sorrow, we had not a grain of quinine to dispense."

The natives believed that this disease had originated from the re-opening of a pit, into which it was stated to have been cast years before. Two native medicine men are said to have gone round every morning, armed with rush baskets, into which they swept *the disease*, and then, after closing the mouth of the baskets, they buried them in deep pits with some powerful charms, using solemn imprecations the while!

In the month of September it was Mr. Pearse's pleasant duty to go down to the coast to meet Mrs. Pearse. It was a merciful Providence that brought Mrs. Pearse out to him before the troubles with the Jesuits came to a head. Mr. and Mrs. Pearse reached their home early in October, to find a condition of universal excitement over the emancipation of the slaves, which had been proclaimed a few days previously. This was one of the last acts of Monsieur Laroche, during his occupancy of the position of Resident-General. Mr. Pearse says: "It has brought freedom to numerous families and joy to many hearts but trouble and sorrow to others. The freed slaves are loud in praise of their liberators but the former owners cannot pass any eulogium on those who have taken their property from them, without giving any compensation, and have thus made the most radical changes necessary in their domestic and family life.   It is impossible not to rejoice with the former, and one cannot but have sympathy also with families thus un-expectedly cast upon their own resources and compelled to perform for themselves all those services in home and ricefield which, through all their previous life, had been done for them by slaves.   So far as my own observation has extended, the Christian population have accepted the position in a quiet and submissive spirit, and express their confidence that the emancipation of their slaves will prove to be among the ' all things ' which will surely work for their good and promote the benefit of the country."

Undoubtedly this has been verified, and the creation of a spirit of greater self-reliance, also the partial ex-tirpation of the foolish pride about doing even the slightest act of menial work, have resulted from this enlightened measure.

CHAPTER XII

Disasters

1896 to 1898

It was in the month of October, 1896, that General Gallieni entered upon his dual offices of Commander of the Army of Occupation and Resident-General of France. His appointment marked the determination of his government to quell the rebellion and substantiate the authority of France, with all the vigour necessary.

The rebellion was a movement amongst the heathen population of Imèrina, who, stung by the ignominy of conquest, rebelled indiscriminately against everything foreign. The foreign army and foreign arms which had vanquished them, the foreign God who had, so they held, naturally aided His own party against them, and incidentally every foreign object, from the Bible, and other books issued by the mission presses, to the clothes, medicines, cups and plates of foreign introduction, were all the objects of their frenzied attack. " Madagascar for the Malagasy " and " down with everything foreign "—those were the rallying cries.

Now a very potent factor in the spread of foreign influence was the work of the London Missionary Society, and naturally that Society suffered particularly, though by no means exclusively, by the aggressions of the rebels. But its power brought antipathy from another quarter, *viz.*, the French government, very properly intent on establishing its own influence as paramount in the island. Thus the society was assailed from both sides.

The influence of the London Missionary Society was not understood by the French ; it was declared to be political, as it was impossible for France to believe that a purely disinterested non-political work could be carried on. The political propagandism of the Jesuit priests had always been very much in evidence, and the realization of this led the authorities to infer that, from their own side, the London Missionary Society would adopt similar projects.

The policy of the government was thus directed against the two powers, supposed to be in antipathy to them, the rebels and the London Missionary Society.

But the London Missionary Society had another opponent. Not only were the government and the rebels against them, but the Jesuit mission was full of triumphant anticipation of bringing them to nought. It is quite easy to see, therefore, how tempting it was for the government to use the unscrupulous ambitions of the Jesuits as a weapon in their own policy of repression.

The country was, at the time, under martial law and the Jesuitical sympathies of some of the military determined the form which the acts of repression so frequently took in Imèrina, viz., attempts by officers to implicate the missionaries in charges of abetting rebellion and to prove their agents and converts guilty of the same offence. To connect their two opponents in this way and try to establish complicity between the London Missionary Society and their adherents, on the one hand, and on the other, the rebels who were killing those adherents and ruthlessly destroying all the churches and other property they could lay their hands on, was not a particularly logical proceeding. Our concern at present, however, is not with Imèrina or North Bètsilèo, where the rebellion was rife, but with South Bètsilèo, on which it laid no hold. The military were not so largely in evidence there but it so happened that the Jesuit sympathies of some of the civil authorities led to the same kind of alliance being made for the destruction of London Missionary Society influence. The Roman Catholic priests, therefore, were exceedingly active in their endeavours to annihilate the work of the English missionaries and a programme of repression was entered upon, of great thoroughness and ingenuity.

The chief incidents in this programme may be briefly enumerated here.

1. As we have already seen, the return of the Resident to Fianàrantsòa was immediately marked by the bringing of serious charges against the London Missionary Society missionaries and the according of conspicuous favour to the Jesuits.

2. Rumours of the most extravagant character were disseminated broadcast, calculated to produce the utmost fear and suspicion in the minds of the natives. Those who attended the Protestant churches and schools were pointed at as being disloyal, and retribution of terrible kinds was predicted.

3. Commencing in December, 1896, the best Hova evangelists were suddenly ordered to return immediately to Imèrina, the central province, without reason given.

4. The adherents of the churches, weakened by the loss of these leaders and frightened by the continual rumours so assiduously disseminated, were ready to fall a prey to the priests and their workers.

5. Any complaints of the missionaries were either

taken no notice of or else turned to the injury of those for whom they pleaded.

6. The congregations having been largely frightened into Catholicism, their churches were then claimed as needed for Catholic worship, and the missionaries were officially informed of this proceeding being contemplated.

7. The question of ownership of churches was ordered by decree of General Gallieni to be settled by a Commission of natives, appointed to go into each dispute and report to him. This measure, fair in its inception, was, however, nullified in its effects by the Commission being packed, as its members were largely perverts from London Missionary Society churches. The *modus operandi* laid down by General Gallieni was departed from, and although very strong and reiterated complaints were made by the missionaries on that account, no attempt was made to be impartial, and the findings of the Commission were, so far as they went, uniformly against the Protestants.

Before the Commission had concluded its sittings, however, the Governor-General decided, as the result of instructions from France, that no church should change hands, consequently this particular action on the part of the Jesuits failed. The policy of dissemination of rumours was carried on, and, in spite of the failure of this attempt, terror filled the minds of those who were still adherents of the London Missionary Society.

8. Almost, if not all, the native officials who were adherents to the London Missionary Society, especially if they were active, were removed and replaced by Roman Catholics. Such of them, however, as embraced Roman Catholicism were allowed to remain.

9. The teaching of French was ordered in all the schools. As it was supposed that the teachers in the

London Missionary Society schools would be unable to meet this demand, advantage was expected to accrue to the Jesuit schools. As it happened, however, the teachers had already been specially prepared in French.

10. The teachers of the London Missionary Society schools, when their scholars had been frightened into leaving them, were taunted with having so few left to teach, and the advantages accorded by the government to teachers, in the way of remission of taxes, were withdrawn in their case.

11. Fines and imprisonment were meted out in unstinting measure to adherents of London Missionary Society churches.

12. Finally, more agents were banished to Imèrina.

This policy was pursued for a period of rather under two years, but the six months between December, 1896, and June, 1897, saw the most active attempts at proselytizing.

At the time of the latter date the members of the Mission Evangélique de Paris were commencing to arrive in Madagascar and a visit by some of them was paid to Fìanàrantsòa in order to render what help they could to Protestantism and to inspire with fresh courage the native Christians who had passed through such trials of persecution for that cause.

After conference with these brethren, the whole of the work of primary education was handed over to their care, and that step, together with the reassuring statements made by them on the subject of the reality of the religious liberty granted by France, served to stem the tide of Jesuit oppression. It was recorded that at these meetings "there were present those who have been imprisoned, fined and paralyzed with fear, listening with breathless attention to what the new-comers had to say and with countenances beaming with light and joy."

The attempt of the French Protestant missionaries to relieve the situation in Bètsilèo was, however, marked by another crushing blow. Two of their number were to visit Fìanàrantsòa and it was hoped that Pasteur Minault would remain there to reinforce the sorely-tried brethren of the London Missionary Society. On their way south, while passing through a lonely part of the country, Messrs. Minault and Benjamin Escande were shot. Concerning the origin of this dastardly crime, the most sinister rumours were afloat, and among those who suffered the death penalty for the murder were several native members of the Roman Catholic communion.

The spirit in which these troubles were met comes out in a letter written at this time by Mrs. Pearse :—" A crisis indeed it is and for us here in the Bètsilèo it seems scarcely possible for the outlook to be darker than it is to-day ; yet the faith of some of us never was stronger. Speaking for myself, I can say that as the clouds have darkened around us, the power to look beyond, to Him who is working out His own plans and ends, has been given. Whatever may be the Master's wise designs in permitting all this, I hope that, on our part, there will be no thought of drawing back. As far as we here are concerned, whatever may be the trials and difficulties we may be called upon to endure, we have no thought of allowing these to drive us from our post. Until we are *compelled* to leave, we shall feel it to be our duty to keep the lamp of Protestantism burning, if only by our presence here. I believe this is required of us, not only for the sake of the Malagasy but for that of the French, who are themselves the blind bondservants of these

Jesuits. Above all, for the Master's sake, who before us endured persecutions."

Mr. Pearse recorded in detail the history of this period in a report sent to the Mission House. He writes :—

" In this statement I have to tell of a large decrease in the number of adults attending our public religious services, of a greatly diminished number of scholars in our schools ; and of some of our out-stations, which at the commencement of the year (1897), were in a most promising condition, but are now absolutely ruined. During recent months the London Missionary Society Mission in South Bètsilèo has been exposed to such formidable and persistent attacks from its allied foes, that the wonder is that it has been saved from complete destruction.

" Not cheerfully nor willingly have the people withdrawn from us, but most of them have done so under the influence of that fear, of which the natives in this part of Madagascar have almost universally become the victims.

" The Malagasy are not an emotional people, but during the past year I have seen women, and men too, weep bitterly on account of what they have considered absolutely necessary separation from us, if they would remain unmolested in their homes and occupations, and avoid the risks of Jesuit and other intrigues.

" To destroy the London Missionary Society work, and to drive its missionaries off the field of their successful labours, certain officials and the Jesuit priests appear to have entered into an alliance, and in carrying on the warfare against us, they have united in action, the one supporting and encouraging the other. The priests, assisted by numerous native agents, have applied themselves to the odious work of destroying our mission with a determination scarcely surpassed in the annals of Jesuit audacity. By various means they have successfully impressed upon the people that to join their churches and schools is to give unequivocal testimony of absolute submission to the French and unhesitating loyalty to the Republic ; while to continue in association with the London Missionary Society missionaries (who have been libellously represented as enemies of France), is an evidence not only of non-submission, but of active opposition to, and rebellion against the rules of the colony.

" Much valuable time has had to be spent in meeting Jesuit craft, boldness and unscrupulousness, and in resisting cunningly-planned attacks and ingeniously-devised surprises.

" At the close of 1896 and the beginning of this year, a bold and successful attempt was made to weaken our churches and schools and to injure our influence and work by the sudden removal of many of the evangelists and other native workers connected with the mission.   These workers were, for the most part, intelligent Hovas, who had resided for many years in this part of Madagascar, while others were younger men, who had been trained in the London Missionary Society's College and schools in Antanànarìvo.   In the space of two months, twenty-eight such workers were peremptorily ordered to leave the province of Bètsilèo within five days and return to Imèrina.   No crime or political charge was laid against them nor were they even told why this sad fate had befallen them.   With one exception, no reason whatever was assigned for their summary conviction.   At later dates, others were similarly treated, and the number of London Missionary Society male workers evicted from Bètsilèo between December, 1896, and June, 1897, reaches the large total of fifty individuals. One of the last was Rajaònimarìa, who had been our evangelist at Nasàndratròny since 1890, and who had been associated with the London Missionary Society as teacher and preacher for more than twenty years.

" This treatment of our best native workers admits of only one interpretation. It has been done to demonstrate the unfavourable manner in which our work and influence are regarded by the authorities, and to weaken our position by causing the people to sever their connection with us from fear of similar treatment being meted out to them.

" In one small town, thus bereft of its evangelist, fear seized upon everyone, and adults and scholars immediately took refuge in the Jesuit fold. On the two Sundays immediately following the departure of the evangelist, no one dared even to open the doors of the London Missionary Society's chapel. I visited the town, but by my most earnest efforts only succeeded in getting about a dozen people to meet me in the chapel. I encouraged them to rally and hold the position and tried to dispel their fears, but it was of no avail. ' See,' they answered, ' what is happening to those who remain in association with the English. We do not go to the Roman Catholics from choice but from fear of what will happen to us if we do not.'

" Further evidence in corroboration of the character of the attack is furnished by the fact that several of our workers, who were officially summoned to appear and who were included among the number of those ordered to leave within five days, were nevertheless allowed to remain when they joined the Jesuit ranks.

" Others of our native workers have been fined, imprisoned, and made to ' serve with rigour,' under various pretexts, and because of false accusations laid against them, which they have not been allowed any opportunity of disproving, and they have been pointed at as illustrations of what others might expect who dared to remain in association with us. A case which came under my personal observation was that of a teacher, who had proved himself upright in his conduct and faithful in his attention to his duties. He had received back several scholars, who, from fear of what might happen to them, had left our school and gone over to that of the Jesuits, but who now ventured to return. Official instructions required that our teacher should notify this fact to the teacher of the Jesuit school. Approaching the Roman Catholic school for that purpose one Sunday morning he was set upon by the other teacher and severely knocked about, in the presence of several members of both congregations. He lodged a complaint with the native Governor-General, and was apparently sympathetically received, and a time was fixed for the Jesuit teacher to answer the charge. The appointed day arrived but the investigation was postponed and postponed again until more than a month had elapsed. Then our teacher was summoned, and to his astonishment, charged with entering the Roman Catholic chapel and disturbing the peace, and the accusation being supported by false witnesses, sentence of banishment was passed and he was ordered to leave within five days. I wrote a detailed account of the circumstances to the Resident and respectfully begged that he might be given an opportunity of producing witnesses and proving his innocence, but no notice was taken of the appeal.

" In the month of February (1897) a new plan of attack was carried into execution and a determined attempt made to obtain possession of no less than ninety-six churches which had been erected in connection with the London Missionary Society and used for Protestant worship and education. Previous attempts made by the Jesuits in Imèrina to obtain possession of London Missionary Society churches, had led General Gallieni to issue an order for the establishment of a native commission to investigate all disputes among the natives concerning the proprietorship of church property. He decreed that 'No compulsion must be brought to bear on the people in connection with the religion they prefer to follow, for they have absolute freedom in their choice. There are those who have opposed my oft-repeated commands and have assumed power to which they have no right, in order to increase by force the numbers of their sect. It is my business to stop this, for it is in opposition to that freedom of choice which all have and which I wish them to enjoy.' The details of this order were most wise and just and calculated to secure a righteous settlement of any disputes which might arise. These details, however, were disregarded and grossly perverted by the commission which was appointed at Fìanàrantsòa. There were four members on that commission, three of whom had, since the French occupation, severed their connection with us and joined the Jesuits. According to the order, the conditions for calling the commission were the existènce of a dispute concerning church property in any town or village and also the receipt of a written appeal from the disputing parties. However, in Bètsilèo, there were no disputes originating from us about the proprietorship of any of the buildings erected by Protestants nor was a single appeal presented to the commission from our members; moreover, it was the Jesuit priests themselves, and not natives (as required by the decree) who handed in the names of these ninety-six churches, which they affirmed their newly-gained adherents laid claim to. This action of the Jesuits was obsequiously accepted by the commission, who forthwith proceeded with their despicable work. Without delay, my fellow-missionaries and myself earnestly protested, by letter and in person, against this course of procedure, as diametrically opposed to General Gallieni's order ; but our protests were disregarded and every appeal was rejected. The issue was inevitable. The verdict of the commission was, of course, in favour of the Jesuits. Within a fortnight a decision that ten of our churches should be handed over to the Jesuits was arrived at, and pending the confirmation of this decision by the General, to whom it had been submitted, a local order was issued for the closing of these churches. Writhing under the gross injustice of the whole procedure and knowing how injurious would be even the temporary closing of the churches, we pleaded that the order might be stayed ; but we pleaded in vain, and the churches were officially closed. Happily, however, the local decision was not confirmed by General Gallieni. After the ten churches had been closed for several weeks and before any judgment had been announced on the remaining eighty-six, a despatch was received from the General, from which the following is an extract :—

" ' I have the honour to bring to your knowledge, that, conformable to the orders contained in a cablegram from the minister for the colonies, I have decided from to-day not to authorize any change in the actual appropriation of religious edifices.'

" After the receipt of that communication, our churches were allowed to be re-opened and the work of the commission ignominiously collapsed. By this time, however, a panic of fear had seized many of our adherents, and many deserted our ranks, who still hesitate to return.

"Our mission has been still further weakened by the removal from office of nearly all the Hova who held official positions in the province and by the pressure which has been, only too successfully, used to induce those who have been appointed as their successors to join the Jesuits. A considerable number of natives occupy positions of varying grades under the French government. Until within the last eighteen months the great majority of these were adherents of the London Missionary Society; now, almost without exception, they call themselves Roman Catholics. To a small extent this may have been on their part a voluntary act, taken from a cringing desire to secure the approbation of their conquerors and the Jesuit priests; but others have undoubtedly been the victims of pressure and Jesuitical tyranny, from which it has been impossible for them to escape and which they have not had the moral courage to resist. As one, whom I had regarded as a steadfast Protestant, expressed it : ' I am obliged to attend the Roman Catholic chapel when I am in Fìanà-rantsòa. Official word has been given me, and whether I wish to do so or not, *I must.*'

"Not only have such direct attacks been aimed at our mission, but the quieter working of all manner of unfavourable and intimidating reports, insidiously and perseveringly spread by the native agents of the Jesuits, has caused even greater disaster to us. The most extravagant reports have been foisted upon the simple-minded and ignorant Bètsilèo, such as the following :—

" ' All who do not join the Roman Catholics are not recognized as French subjects.'

" ' All recently freed slaves found in the Protestant congregations will be brought back into slavery, if they do not join the Romanists.'

" ' All the Protestant churches are about to be destroyed by the French authorities, and, after that, those who remain Protestant will be shot.'

" ' A conscription of soldiers is about to take place. No Roman Catholics will be enrolled, but only those who continue to be associated with the English missionaries.'

" ' All who do not join the Romanists before June 27th will be fined twelve shillings and sent to prison."

" The ingenuity of our opponents to create and circulate such false and malicious slanders has been marvellous. The original birth-place of such reports has certainly not been the native Bètsilèo mind.

"Christians at home, strong through the nurture of years of education and moral and religious influences, will perhaps criticize adversely the ready manner in which many of our Bètsilèo have yielded to such basely fabricated and intimidating reports, and be inclined to censure them for their groundless fears ; but I would plead for gentleness and the greatest forbearance towards them in this matter. The Bètsilèo are but as infants, who start at any unfamiliar form or sound, and their moral strength must be measured by a different standard from that which is applied to European Christians, who have learned from history the unscrupulous manner and tyrannical despotism of the Jesuit fathers, and the persecuting spirit of the Church of Rome.

" The cablegram received from the French Colonial Minister and the official proclamations which have been made to the people from time to time, forbid any doubt that it is the sincere desire of the French Government that the Malagasy should have religious liberty. The following declaration on freedom of conscience and religious toleration appeared in 1896 :—

" ' Les protestants, les catholiques, les diverses communions, leurs écoles, jouiront d'une égale protection sous nos lois ; et il serait contraire à nos mœurs d'en favoriser une, à plus forte raison de la persécuter."

" Nothing could be more satisfactory than that declaration thus officially and publicly made by Monsieur Laroche and subsequently confirmed on several occasions by General Gallieni. We gladly recognize the position taken as being to the honour of the great nation which has become the foster-parent of the Malagasy and it is profoundly to be regretted that anything has been allowed to eclipse that honour. Such has, however, alas! been the case. It has been done in Bètsilèo, where I unhesitatingly affirm that religious liberty has not been enjoyed during many months. From a considerable number of the most intelligent and trustworthy persons I know in the province of Bètsilèo, I asked a written reply to the question : " Why have so many people separated from the London Missionary Society ? ' and, without a single exception, the answer was, ' *From fear.*'

" Even idolatry and the superstitious customs of the Malagasy have received greater encouragement than the Protestant mission, for an official notice was promulgated granting " the fullest liberty to make (or possess) idols (or charms) according to their old customs, or even to employ sorcery, for they are not opposed to the laws of the colony.' This proclamation was the more remarkable in that the possession of all such things as were above enumerated had been expressly forbidden by a proclamation early in 1896.

" The weakness which many of our adherents have shown

has been sad to witness, whatever may be brought forward in extenuation, and the disappointment which certain professing Christians have caused us has been very keen.   There have not been wanting, however, instances of real fortitude, which have been most encouraging and inspiring, and the severe ordeal through which our mission has recently passed has brought to light true nobleness and sincerity of Christian character on the part of some.

"At Kàlamavòny, where the Hova governor has signalized himself by hypocrisy, servility and tyranny over those under his command, there lived a young teacher and his wife whose conduct and endurance were admirable.   Under the coercion and intimidation of the governor, after he had deserted the London Missionary Society and joined the Roman Catholics, the whole of the large congregation followed him, with the exception of this young couple, and when, soon after, the governor joined in league with the Jesuits to obtain possession of the large London Missionary Society church, they had the courage to stand forth in the presence of the assembled population and protest against the misappropriation of the Protestant building.

"Another young man, an evangelist, who was falsely accused and imprisoned, after telling in a letter from his prison-house of the excessive weight of the irons with which he and his companions were loaded, added : 'Trust still in God, for whatever is done is a test and discipline used by God for working our good.'

"On the afternoon of the first Sunday in May, while our congregation of Ambòhimandròso was dispersing, twenty-two men were arrested at the chapel door, several of whom had, in the morning, received the Lord's Supper for the first time.   Sixteen of the number (the majority quite youths) were afterwards imprisoned. During the following months, these youths, with their heads shorn, and in prison garb, were frequently seen going to, and returning from, the ' hard labour ' which was part of their sentence. To meet them, as we occasionally did, was quite an inspiration, for their countenances shone brightly, and their whole bearing told that they were enduring joyfully, and with Christian courage and patience, the unjust sentence passed upon them because of their association with our missionaries. One afternoon the mother of three of the youths called on us. After giving a detailed account of what her sons had to do and bear, which roused our warm sympathy, she said: ' But the Master had to endure far heavier trials. His hands and feet were pierced with nails. His head was crowned with thorns. He suffered unto death.'

"For these native friends, and others like them, we magnify the grace of God. They are our confidence for the present and our hope for the future, and make us not ashamed of our boasting concerning the success which has attended the teaching of the word of God and the preaching of the gospel in this part of Madagascar. Thank God, something has by His grace and blessing been done, which is bearing fruit to His glory, in these unfavourable and testing times."

A fuller account of the thanksgiving service held at Nasàndratròny to celebrate the re-opening of the church is given in Mr. Pearse's own words :

" Nasàndratròny, which is one of the chief places in the Isàndra division of Bètsilèo, has been an out-station in connection with the London Missionary Society for more than twenty years, and during the last few years the educational and spiritual work carried on there, under the superintendence of our excellent evangelist, Rajaò-nimarìa, has been most encouraging and full of promise. In the centre of the village stands one of the neatest, most substantial and best finished churches in Bètsilèo, towards the erection of which the native contributions amounted to about forty-six pounds. It was far too important a position for the Jesuits to pass by with indifference, and accordingly, out of the ninety-six churches which, during the month of March, they laid siege to and planned to obtain possession of, this was among the first actually attacked.

" The enemy's cunningly-laid plans were so far successful, that, notwithstanding our most strenuous opposition, a letter was addressed to us by the native Governor-General informing us, that, as a majority of the people in the village had left the Protestant communion, it had been decided that our church should be passed over to the Roman Catholics. He also told us that he had issued an order for the building to be closed, pending the confirmation of the local decision by General Gallieni. In conformity with that order, the door of our church was locked and for five Sundays, the Protestants gathered for their services in the evangelist's house. On one of those Sundays, Mrs. Pearse paid them a visit, and I was with them on another. In due time, the answer of the General to the communication about the ownership of the churches was received in Fìanàrantsòa. This, which was very different from what our enemies desired or anticipated, has already been quoted.

" The receipt of this was a great relief and cause of abounding joy to us. Without delay I communicated the good news to our friends at Nasàndratròny, and asked them to arrange for a special service in connection

with the re-opening of the church. In his reply the
evangelist said: ' We join in thanking God for His
gracious favour. He has touched the hearts of those
in authority. Praise the Lord, for His mercy is everlasting ! I am very glad that God has granted us, His
servants, the victory, and protected the honour of His
name.'

" I reached the village about ten a.m. on Saturday,
April 17th (1897), and, soon after, the bell was rung
and a company of the Protestants having assembled,
the key was produced and the door unlocked, and we
re-entered the church which our enemies had so
confidently expected to obtain possession of that they
had made preparations for an opening service to signalize
their victory.

" Our service was simple and undemonstrative but
the countenances of our small congregation beamed with
joy, and the expressions of one and another told of the
fervent gratitude which filled their hearts. We commenced with the hymn, ' Misaòra, an' i Zànahàry,'
which corresponds in sentiment and familiarity with
our own ' All people that on earth do dwell.'

" Rajaònimarìa the evangelist then read the official
letter authorizing the re-opening of the church, after
which he called to the congregation : ' I wish you all to
join with me in saying " Long live France." ' To this
there was an immediate and hearty response and the
people simultaneously gave the acclamation in their
own language. It was a spontaneous and interesting
feature in the service, and shows how the Protestants
appreciate the just treatment they have received at the
hands of the French government, the influence of which
will, I am sure, be most favourable in helping the Bètsilèo
to realize that France is indeed seeking their welfare.

"Continuing the service I read various short portions
of scripture, among others: 'The Lord executeth righteous acts and judgment for all that are oppressed.'
'The Lord upholdeth all that fall and raiseth up all that
be bowed down.' 'He will fulfil the desire of them that
fear Him; He also will hear their cry and will save
them.' We then united in thanksgiving and prayer,
and rededicated the church to Him, for whose worship,
according to the Protestant faith, it was originally
erected, and also again consecrated ourselves humbly
to His service. Brief addresses of exhortation and
encouragement followed, and then with another hymn
we brought this novel service to a close.

"The modes of action recently adopted by the Jesuits
have not deepened the native respect for them; and
evidence is not wanting that, simple-minded, fearful
and easily beguiled as many of the Bètsilèo are, their
eyes are being opened to the insincerity of the many
intimidating statements so frequently circulated by the
native agents of the Jesuits. Said an old Bètsilèo quite
recently: 'Through fear I left the Protestants and
joined the Roman Catholics, and I took my five children
with me. Shortly afterwards the report was circulated
that very soon the Resident was coming to shoot all the
people who did not go over to the Roman Catholics.
I waited for this to take place, but nothing came of it.
Then it was said that all the Protestant churches were
to be burned down. Again I watched for that to take
place, but not one has been burned. Then it was
reported that all the Protestant churches were to be
taken possession of and the missionaries sent away, and
that this was the reason why the churches had not been
destroyed by fire. I waited for the fulfilment of this,'
continued the old man, 'but, lo! once more nothing

came of it. My conclusion is that all that has been
reported (to frighten and influence us) is false ; and not
being willing to be imposed upon, I have gone back with
my five children to the Protestants.' "

In the month of September, Mr. Pearse left for Antanànarìvo in order to meet the London Missionary Society
deputation, Rev. R. Wardlaw Thompson and Alderman
Evan Spicer, and escort them on their visit to the
Bètsilèo mission. He stayed for some days at Ambòsitra,
the station formerly occupied by Mr. and Mrs. Brockway, and made arrangements for the settling in there of
a missionary of the French Protestant Society. At
one village he records that " the wife of a native pastor
came claiming acquaintance with me. She reminded
me that she was first a scholar and then a teacher in
the school at Anàlakèly. She spoke very gratefully of
spiritual good received in those days. She is now the
mother of a large family, and engaged with her husband
in Christian work, but their work had been much
interfered with and their persons in danger during the
rebellion."

At Antanànarìvo, where he arrived on October 1st, he
was warmly welcomed, not only by his daughter, then
residing there, but by many old friends among the
missionary circle and a very large number of natives.
After preaching once more at Anàlakèly, he records : " The
people expressed very great pleasure in seeing me again
after the long period of sixteen years." He visited some
of his old churches in the country and fulfilled many
other engagements ; he was present also at a long and
interesting series of committee meetings held after the
arrival of the deputation. On 9th November he left
with Mr. Thompson and Mr. Spicer, and arrived at
Fìanàrantsòa once more, on the 17th. He was cheered

to note an improvement in the attendance at several of the gatherings held after his return and welcomed that as an indication that the worst of the storm was over.

At the important committee meetings held during the visit of the deputation, a decision was come to which involved a great change in Mr. and Mrs. Pearse's arrangements. The district of Isàndra, in which they had been interested for so many years, was to be handed over to the French Protestants. It was considered best for the general interests of the work that the French brethren should have a church and district of their own, but while the district of Isàndra was handed over, the mother church of Antrànobiriky was retained and one of the two other churches was given up instead.

This decision, though acquiesced in by Mr. Pearse, could not fail to give him and Mrs. Pearse much sadness in the prospect of removal, but the spirit in which they took it is well displayed in a letter to them from Mr. Thompson, in which he says : " The calm thoughtfulness for others and apparent putting aside of your own cares in a time of peculiar trial of feeling, was a lesson to me. I rejoice with you that you are both able with such quiet confidence to lean upon the love and guidance, and to be assured of the absolutely wise and constant care of God. I felt that you had both learned the secret of which we can all *speak*, of leaving yourselves with perfect assurance in His hands. I shall cherish the remembrance of my visit to you with thankfulness and with pleasure."

From the time of that decision onward there is but little to relate. A few entries of an encouraging nature are to be found in the midst of records of engagements : " The severity of the storm which has swept over the Bètsilèo mission seems to have passed, the persecution is relaxing and the sun is beginning to shine forth from the dark clouds." "The natives are beginning to come about us again a little more, and there are some evidences that the anti-London Missionary Society spirit is not quite so cruel and severe as it was a few months ago."

As the news of the approaching departure of Mr. and Mrs. Pearse became known, there was much feeling of sorrow. "Some of the references made by the natives to our anticipated leaving are very touching and they find it hard to repress their feelings of deep sorrow." Then came certain meetings in Fìanàrantsòa and in the district, at which the announcement was publicly made, and in the latter case, the French missionary who was to be Mr. Pearse's successor was introduced, Pasteur Bénézech. This gentleman, after taking over the work, made the following references to what he found and to his admiration for the workers: "I feel that the religious work which has been carried on here has been very solid. These native teachers and some others, who have remained faithful in a time when terror has been skilfully spread everywhere, are an evident proof that the Malagasy do not change their religion so easily as some people like to say. In the three districts more than 1,000 children and 1,200 grown-up persons have come back to us." And then of Mr. Pearse he says: "I cannot help feeling very sad in realizing that the Bètsilèo work is going to lose such a man. He has a very special talent in speaking the language. His hearers listen to him with the greatest pleasure. He is a popular and distinguished author, who knows how to lead others, and who has the power of attracting men by his energy and indomitable activity. In their relations with the Malagasy, Mr. and Mrs. Pearse have gained all hearts by their amiability, and the circum-

190 A Pioneer in Madagascar

stances which necessitate their departure must be profoundly regretted. They do not say much about it, though it is with very sad hearts that they leave. They do not show much of what they feel. The same happy smile is always seen on their faces, but we know that this departure is tearing the souls of these ardent missionaries." Mr. Pearse introduced M. Bénézech to the people, and recited several striking mottoes which he made the children and their parents repeat several times, e.g., " Have confidence in France ; love her ; listen to and obey her commands ; " and, in addition, he made several eulogistic remarks about France. " My own countrymen," adds M. Bénézech, " could not have spoken better, and one feels, although his words were so strong, they were undoubtedly sincere."

A couple of extracts from letters will reveal the secret of their calmness in this time of trial and unsettlement : " Occasionally we cannot help some feelings of sorrow overtaking us, but at the same time we are *being kept* wonderfully calm and happy in mind. We *know* that ' all things work together for good ' and that our times are in our heavenly Father's hands. Don't be anxious about us or sorry for us. *All is well*."

" There is very much that is good and joy-giving in this world, for which we may exclaim, ' Bless the Lord,' but the *best* is over the line which separates the seen from the unseen. We have had a very good time at Fìanàrantsòa and if we could have followed our own likes and convenience, would have certainly stayed on here till we returned to England. Many hearts besides ours are sad about it, but we mean to be brave, and if we cannot *see* it, we can and do believe that ' All things work together for good.' "

The time of departure was actually the 14th April,
Mr. and Mrs. Pearse had been the recipients of very
warm resolutions passed by their missionary brethren
in committee, and on separating from them, he says :
" The sorrow on the part of all was sincere and heavy."
In a letter he records : " It was a great sorrow to our
friends in Bètsilèo and to us to sever the close and happy
bonds by which we were united. God has been very
gracious to us in giving strength, as we have needed it
from day to day, in what has been a season of very
heavy trial to us. We are now looking forward boldly
and happily to our unknown and uncertain future."

CHAPTER XIII

A Visit to Antsihànaka

1898

MR. PEARSE had cherished the hope that possibly he might be able to recommence the mission in Antsihànaka which had been relinquished during the war. The general circumstances of the London Missionary Society did not lead the brethren to encourage him in that course, but they were prepared to sanction a visit by Mr. and Mrs. Pearse to that province in order to examine into and report upon its condition.

On their arrival, therefore, at Antanànarìvo, no time was wasted, but they proceeded at once with the needful preparations. They were much cheered by a cordial interview with General Gallieni and by his spontaneous offer of his card, wherewith to overcome difficulties that might arise on the journey down.

In a fortnight they were ready to start, and so found themselves once more on the familiar track to the north. Familiar, and yet there were sad changes only too evident, for much of the district had been overrun by the rebels and many of the villages and the promising churches erected in them reduced to ruins ; the country was depopulated, and whatever people there were, were very shy of having anything to do with the missionary ; the district was also famine stricken. On arrival at Ambàtondrazàka they were unable to occupy the house

they had   lived in, as the military were in residence
there.   Mr. Pearse says : " No house had been prepared
for us, although the pastor had received my letter asking
them to do so.   We had to stand about in the public
thoroughfare while a place was sought for us.   By dark
we found ourselves in a fairly large and comfortable
native house " ; and, next day, " A good number of our
old friends have been to see us.   Many have passed away,
and many more have left the place.   Our first impressions are discouraging and decidedly unfavourable."
After a week's stay they left in order to visit a formerly
important station on the shores of the lake, but they
had a great difficulty in getting bearers to carry them,
nearly all the men being engaged in government
service.   Once off, they arrived after one night at
Imèrimandròso, and the diary records : " We have
found a temporary resting place, in a fairly good but
small Sihànaka house, in a good position and commanding an extensive view of the lake.   Rajàofèra
and his wife (a native evangelist who has continued
at his work here for twenty years) and a few of our old
native friends who remain here gave us a very hearty
welcome and expressed great pleasure in seeing us again."
   Conversation with the natives soon put them into
possession of the main incidents connected with the
recent rebellion.   About this, Mr. Pearse wrote : " The
leaders of the rebellion were thoroughly heathen at
heart, and they were urged forward in their evil course
by the confidence they placed in their superstitions, their
charms and their gods, to secure for them the success
of their designs ; and they were, perhaps, quite as
anxious to revive the almost decayed reign of superstition and idolatry as to restore the independence of their
country.   They bedecked their own persons with charms,

varied and numerous, and imperatively commanded
their followers to imitate their example. Just to the
east of our temporary home, there still stands in the
open thoroughfare the god they set up in this village,
and to which they demanded that universal homage
should be paid. Around this the crowd assembled,
and with vociferous shouting, and frenzied dancing,
they made their vows and announced their designs.
One mourns over the awful darkness which enshrouded
the native mind, that to such an object as this god the
smallest amount of respect could have been shown.
There is nothing whatever attractive about it, or calculated to inspire feelings of veneration, confidence or
fear. It consists simply of a young tree brought from
the near forest, with a small stockade of short poles
around it, on the points of which the heads of two
oxen slain in sacrifice were impaled. To this the poor
people addressed themselves as their saviour from
their calamities.

"Notwithstanding the unhesitating steps and the
fanatical boldness with which the rebel bands moved
forwards towards Ambàtondrazàka, their gods proved to
be neither 'gods of the hills' nor 'gods of the valleys,'
and their easy defeat by a very small number of French
troops has had the opposite effect to that which was
desired. Instead of the ancient superstitious customs
and idolatries being revived, I am assured that the
confidence of the Sihànaka in such vanities has been
greatly shaken and more than ever they are feeling after
the living and true God.   'If our gods could have done
anything, they had their opportunity, but they proved
absolutely impotent to help' is a remark which has
been made to us more than once."

A careful report was duly prepared, and sent off to the

capital as soon after their arrival as possible, but Mr. Pearse says about it : " It has had to be done under very unfavourable circumstances and amidst many interruptions. A corner of a small rush hut, in which we have to do everything but cook our food, does not make a study where inspiring thoughts and words come very freely to the mind " ; but the report nevertheless is an able and important document.

I. The Condition of the Antsihànaka Province.

" The movement seems to have commenced in the west, and, from that direction, those who were already in open rebellion came into the province to seek for allies. In this they were only too successful, for *all* the inhabitants of the province joined with the exception of those in Ambàtondrazàka and a few other places. They did this, not perhaps from any true or intelligent sympathy with the rebels and their movement, but because of the coercion which was exercised, and in order to secure their personal safety. All who hesitated to obey the peremptory summons of the rebels to join them, or refused to swear allegiance and fidelity to their cause, were threatened with immediate death.

"The effects of this rebellion have been very sad. As the rebel bands moved from place to place through the province, they destroyed and pillaged many of the villages, and took possession of the herds of cattle which grazed on the plains, which were the wealth of the Sihànaka and of the Hovas who lived among them, and upon which the people depended for working their extensive rice fields. Many hundreds of these cattle were slain and eaten by the rebels and their followers, and thousands were also driven away. One Sihànaka woman told us that she lost a thousand oxen, and her

case is by no means a singular one. The immediate
consequence of the rebellion has been a severe and
widespread famine in the land. Whereas in the years
during which we lived at Ambàtondrazàka, rice was so
abundant that it had hardly any commercial value, in
the early months of this year, the fill of an empty
Swiss-milk tin of white rice sold for tenpence !
Even to-day, what we could have bought in unlimited
quantities in the past for twopence, cannot be had for
less than four shillings ! At one part of our journey
here it was distressing to look upon the emaciated and
feeble bodies of the children, and to find families with
nothing to eat but unwholesome roots and fruits gathered
from the bush and forest.

"The population of Antsihànaka, has, I think, de-
creased considerably. My estimate of it in former
years was 40,000 people ; now, from what I see and hear,
it probably does not reach 30,000.

"One district over which it takes more than two days
to travel by palanquin, is now practically uninhabited.
The French military 'postes' stand out prominently
here and there on the summit of the hills, but during the
whole of this part of our journey, we found nothing but
two or three insignificant villages, and we did not observe
a single head of cattle.

II. The Present Condition of the London
Missionary Society's Mission.

"The French commandant at Ambàtondrazàka, while
admitting that I was absolutely free to visit any parts
of the Antsihànaka province I wished to, yet thought it
right to tell me that, in his opinion, it would not be
prudent to go much into the villages, on account of the
continued unsettled relation of the people to one

another. I felt it becoming and wise to listen to him on this point, and consequently my personal observation on the state of our mission is limited to the region east of the lake Alaòtra and as far north as Imèrimandròso. This is the most important and the most populous part of Antsihànaka ; and I have been able, I think, to obtain pretty accurate information about other parts.

"The result of my information and enquiry is as follows :

" 1.   Throughout the whole of the province there are now no chapels worthy of the name in existence.

"Before the close of the war, most praiseworthy efforts to provide suitable buildings were made by the people, encouraged and superintended by the missionaries. At Ambàtondrazàka, an excellent brick chapel was commenced, the walls finished, and the wood for the roof ready for raising into position. At this period, the crisis in Malagasy history overtook the people and paralyzed all efforts to carry forward this building to completion. Since then, nothing whatever has been done to it ; and it is sad to see it standing thus unfinished and useless, and going gradually to ruin, in a prominent position in the centre of the town of Ambàtondrazàka.

"One village chapel was ruthlessly destroyed by the rebels when on the eve of being opened, another had all the doors and windows torn from it and was otherwise damaged. This has since been roofed and thatched by government orders, and is now used as a government school, the small congregation of Protestants being allowed to worship in it on Sundays.

" 2.   Throughout the province, there are to-day only two places where congregations assemble, Ambàton-drazàka and Imèrimandròso.

"(a) Ambàtondrazàka.—Here there has, so far as I can learn, happily been no break in the meeting of a small number of people for Christian worship every Sunday. When the old chapel of my time was pulled down to make room for the erection of the new one the large school house was selected as a temporary place for assembling in, and here the congregation continues to meet. This school house has been taken possession of by the French government and is now used daily as a school. On the ground, I presume, that it is now claimed as a government building we were not permitted to enter it to join with the people in their services on the Sunday we spent at Ambàtondrazàka. On the Friday after our arrival, the young Protestant Hova who is teacher and superintendent of education, was sent for by the commandant and told : 'The Malagasy are free to gather there for worship as they have been accustomed to do ; but no European may enter the building, whether Pasteurs, Protestant, or Roman Catholic.' This being communicated to us, we contented ourselves with conversing with the few people who came to see us in our temporary home. I was informed that the congregation numbered about sixty in the morning, and about forty in the afternoon.

"(b) Imèrimandròso. Rajàofèra, the long-tried and faithful evangelist at this station, being warned by a Christian Sihànaka woman of the near approach of the rebels, and of the danger to which he exposed his life should he be overtaken by them, secretly left here with his wife, in July, 1896, and took refuge at Ambàtondrazàka. He was away five months, and during that interval no services for Christian worship were held at Imèrimandròso. Immediately on his return, he re-commenced religious services, gathering the people together in his own dwelling-house. Since the date when the church damaged by the rebels was made suitable for assembling in, that has been used for Sunday services. Last Sunday morning there was, I understand, a congregation of about eighty adults.

"3. Throughout the province there are now no evangelists in connection with the London Missionary Society. Those formerly connected with our work have all left the province, with the exception of Rajàofèra, who joined us in 1878, and was placed by me at Tsàrahonènana, and who is now at Imèrimandròso, and another.

"Of Rajàofèra, I feel it impossible to speak too highly. He has given to the London Missionary Society more than twenty years of faithful service, and has kept at his post in this fever district in a truly commendable manner.

"I cannot refrain from expressing my regret that I fail to learn of any effort having been made to retain the services of our evangelists among the Sihànaka. Their connection with us seems to have been broken off, one hardly knows how, or why ; and this, added to the necessary withdrawal of every missionary from Antsihànaka, has caused us to lose what nominal hold we had on the people. Our influence over them cannot be easily regained, and the present condition of the mission is most deplorably weak. This has given some advantage to those who are by no means anxious for our presence here.

"4. Throughout the province there are now neither schools nor teachers connected with the London Missionary Society.

"The educational work was at one time a very successful department of the Antsihànaka Mission. Those of

the Sihànaka who now occupy the highest positions
under the French flag were scholars in the school at
Ambàtondrazàka when we lived and laboured there ;
and many are the expressions of grateful acknowledgment of benefits received in education from our
missionaries, which it has been our pleasure to listen
to, from both men and women, during this visit.
During the rebellion, our mission schools were, with the
single exception of that at Ambàtondrazàka, all broken
up, and everything connected with education either
destroyed, or most carefully concealed by the owners.

"After the rebellion was quelled, but little effort seems
to have been made to revive our mission schools.   Perhaps it was not possible to do anything.   In the autumn
of last year, General Gallieni gave orders to his officers
to establish schools throughout the Antsihànaka
province, and three well-educated Hóva young men
have been sent from Imèrina, in the service of the
French government, to superintend the schools thus
established.

"These young men have other teachers under them,
and they have the superintendence of the central and
district schools.   A large number of children have been
enrolled as scholars, and attend the schools.   At
Imèrimandròso, the average attendance, drawn from the
near villages, is about 400.   The education imparted is
strictly secular—religious teaching of every kind and
faith being forbidden by the authorities.

III. The Claims and Needs of Antsihànaka

"It would be false to affirm that there is to-day any
distinct cry raised by the Sihànaka, saying: "Come
over and help us " ; but their claims to Christian pity,
sympathy, and help, surely deserve serious attention.

From the time of my first acquaintance with them, I have never known a Sihànaka oppose the gospel. Their position has been, and alas ! too universally continues to be, one of apathy and absolute indifference to religion and spiritual things. The non-success of the sad rebellion, in connection with which idolatry and ancient superstition were brought very prominently forward, has loosened the hold and influence of such things on the native mind. The missionaries who have lived and laboured among the Sihànaka, are gratefully and affectionately remembered by many with whom we have come in contact during this visit ; and I believe that the Sihànaka would not only tolerate missionaries among them again, but that some of them would heartily welcome their return ; not indeed, primarily for the spiritual good which it would be their chief desire and aim to impart, but for the medical and other benefits which they might confer."

How terribly saddening must this state of affairs have been to the writer, who had left so promising a work years before!

The opinions formed so soon after arrival in Antsi-hànaka were abundantly verified by more prolonged residence. It was, in many respects, a case of Bètsilèo over again. There were ways of thwarting mission work that made it quite evident that, at that particular time, any forward movement of the London Missionary Society in that direction was inadvisable. Favours granted with one hand were annulled with the other, and very frequently, the local magnate, endowed with "a little brief authority" proved himself exceedingly jealous, not of his rights, which Mr. Pearse was most scrupulous in acknowledging and duly respecting, but of what he considered his rights and powers, which were not always the same thing.

It came to this, that though the usual services in the places of worship were permitted, no European was allowed to be present there; then those who received, or helped, or showed themselves friendly to the Pearses were visited with the displeasure of the above-named authorities; finally, the evangelist was sent away at fourteen days' notice. By these means it was borne in upon Mr. Pearse's mind that, even for the sake of the natives, he must leave as soon as possible. A few allusions to the diary will indicate how the time was employed. "We walked out together to Ambàton-drazàka and managed to get up some little conversation." "Conducted the morning service." "Operated on an ugly swelling on a man's foot." "Was informed that I was no longer free to conduct services in the chapel on Sundays. The natives could continue to assemble there, but I was not allowed to gather with them. In reading out of 'The Heart of Midlothian' last evening, we came across this passage: 'We are in the hands of Ane that kens better what is gude for us than we ken what is for oursells.'" "Not being allowed to conduct service in the chapel, we walked to a near village, where we talked with the people and had a simple service in a native house." "Walked to one of the villages on the border of the lake. A few people gathered round us, and we had the opportunity of reading to them the parable of the prodigal son and a few other striking gospel verses." "Removed into a larger and more convenient house." "I have taken on a patient, who is *very* ill." "Called away to see a man said to be *very* ill, a short distance off. Recovery very doubtful. The former patient is getting on famously."

" *July* 1st.—The month opens with clouds rising, which
threaten to disappoint our hopes of being able to do a
little to re-establish this wrecked mission. The good
man who allowed us to hold our brief, simple service
in his house has been sent to help in making roads and
likewise the owner of the larger house into which
we have moved. The people regard this as a punish-
ment and are more afraid than ever to let it be seen that
they have any communications with us." "Another
day of enforced inactivity in the Master's service. A
few children gathered ; Mrs. Pearse showed them some
scripture pictures, and had a little talk with them.
Went to a hamlet where I have had a patient very ill.
In God's mercy he is better. He and his family (truly
with us in heart) expressed much gratitude." "Acted
as surgeon." "Our evangelist, Rajàofèra, was told
to leave with his wife within eight days ; the time was
however extended to a fortnight. No charges are laid
against him." "Mrs. Pearse visited a poor paralyzed
girl to whom she had given a Bible. On asking where
it was, the girl replied : ' I have hidden it, for the sergeant
came in and was angry with me when he found me
reading it.' " "Since Rajàofèra's summons, increasing
fear has taken hold of the poor natives." "On Sunday,
the natives held a service but I am told that they could
not manage to sing through even one hymn, but after
attempting several, were obliged to give up, because
of their inability to restrain their grief at the expulsion
of Rajàofèra." "Rajàofèra and his wife left during
the morning, to the great regret and amidst the sup-
pressed sorrow of the people, among whom they have
lived and worked for more than twenty years. They
each kissed our hands, when saying ' good-bye,' and were
much affected, although they are both bearing their

unjust treatment bravely.   Very few to visit us to-day.
One or two sick folk ventured in, after looking carefully
round to see that no one was looking."

"*Sunday.*—No opportunity for any work.   Hardly
anyone coming near us."   Mahomet in an hour of
difficulty and trial had only, we are told, one of his
comrades with him, who tremblingly said : ' We are only
two.'   Mahomet's courage rose ; he replied : ' There is
another, there is God.' "

" And in heaven all dark places will be made light ;
all mysteries, mercifully veiled below, will be explained
away for ever ;   every ' wherefore ' will be answered ;
all the agonies of earth, forgotten ; all its weariness,
ended ; its heartache exchanged for joy and rest, which
shall endure for evermore."

Thus, in the midst of so much of a galling and depress-
ing character, Mr. and Mrs. Pearse were able to retain
their composure ; and the ability to discover and appropriate the lessons of such quotations as the above was
one of the things that helped them to overcome this
great disappointment.

But the time was soon made clear to them for their
return to Antanànarìvo.   Mr. and Mrs. Sharman had
been ordered away to Europe on account of the serious
illness of the latter.   The work they were called upon
to relinquish consisted of the charge of a district and
school, as well as, in Mrs. Sharman's case, that of a boy's
home which had been a very successful and promising
undertaking.   The superintendence of these departments
was proposed to Mr. and Mrs. Pearse and in response to
the pathetic appeal made on behalf of the boys by Mrs.
Sharman, they readily consented to become responsible
for that work if a little experience of it warranted their
continuance.   A reply was therefore sent to the capital

by heliograph, bearers were despatched to fetch Mr. and Mrs. Pearse, and by the end of August they were once more in Antanànarìvo, prepared to throw themselves into these new responsibilities, and glad to bring to a termination their very trying visit to Antsihànaka.

CHAPTER XIV

Ripe Experience

1898 to 1902

Of the educational work devolving upon Mr. Pearse in his new sphere it is not necessary to say much; the following record indicates its character: "To-day I commenced my new work by going to the school at eight o'clock and remaining there till one p.m. Such are to be my hours there on five days every week. As our Normal school building was taken by the government, the school is now held in the Ampàmarìnana Memorial Church and adjacent buildings (pending the erection of a new building). The number of scholars present was 197. Nearly all the teaching is done in the French language, so that I shall not be able to do anything so far as practical teaching is concerned, except indeed Scripture teaching, which is still done in Malagasy."

It was the general superintendence and keeping of discipline which he was responsible for, but it was quite evident that the reputation of the school did not suffer in his hands, because the attendance grew to something over 300, before the time came for him to relinquish it.

The district work involved the charge of one of the churches in the capital, viz., Isòtry, and the superintendence of the country stations connected with it; these, however, were at a distance of four or five hours'

journey and it was thus impossible for him to pay
frequent visits ; the plan adopted was to go down into
the district every few months and spend some days there,
travelling by palanquin from one village to another.
One of these occasions is recorded pretty fully in the
diary, and an interesting account of his experience is
given.

" *March* 18*th*, 1899.—Left home about 7 a.m. Fortunately a fine morning, after days and days of dull,
wet weather. Took my lunch at noon, under the shade
of a tree outside a small village, while my men cooked
and ate their rice in one of the small huts. Further on
we came to the village where lives the French captain
in charge of the district. I called on him to pay my
respects, and to inform him of my purpose to pass a few
days in his district, visiting the churches, etc. He
received me very graciously and we spent a short time
in conversation on general matters. I reached my
headquarters before dark and settled down for the
night in a small house occupied by the evangelist.
Before the evening meal we had a gathering of those
near for evening prayers ; a French corporal attended.

" *March* 19*th, Sunday.*—Had talk with the evangelist
and pastor about various matters affecting the church
and work. The chapel has come to grief during the
rainy season, and so, of course, the rebuilding of it had
to be considered. Then, accompanied by the evangelist,
I visited two of the stations under his superintendence
and conducted simple services at each. I am passing
the night at a fairly comfortable house, with an upper
story, where I do not find ' creeping things ' or hopping
things so numerous as is sometimes the case in the
native dwellings. The whole of this district was desolated by the rebels soon after the close of the war, and

the chapels at the two stations I have visited to-day were both burned by them.

"*Monday.*—After my morning meal, started for a village, where I found a very neat and suitable chapel, in which a congregation of about eighty folk were gathered, awaiting my arrival. I preached in simple language from the words : ' This man receiveth sinners.' At the close of the service I was invited to adjourn to a hut near, in which I found a dinner prepared for me and the evangelist—rice, milk, and meat as tough as leather, to bite and eat which was a feat quite impossible to me.

"*Tuesday.*—On to another neat chapel and found a goodly number of people waiting; spoke on : ' God is love.' A simple feast had been prepared, which was spread and partaken of in the chapel. A journey of about six miles brought me to the station of another evangelist, under whose roof I am passing the night. At the place where we were this morning the Roman Catholics have recently erected a chapel within fifty feet of ours.

"*Wednesday.*—With the evangelist and his wife to a place two hours' journey off and conducted service, afterwards going on to another, for a second service. In the evening at an important station. The evangelist was in the north, but when the rebellion broke out was obliged to leave, as his life was in danger ; he and his wife are sterling characters. Last night the mosquitoes made a fierce attack upon me ; to-night the fleas are preparing to follow up the assault and finish me !

"*Thursday.*—The ' hoppers ' had a grand time of it, and consequently I experienced little of the poet's ' balmy sleep.' The day has been spent pleasantly and, I hope, usefully. We had services morning and

THE PASTORS OF ANTANÀNARÌVO CHURCHES.

afternoon, and the people listened attentively. I have
had interesting conversation with one woman in particular, who evinces sincere sorrow for her husband, because,
as she said, ' he is not a Christian.'

" *Friday.*—Had a small gathering in a native hut,
as the chapel was blown down by the wind a few months
ago. I am in another evangelist's house ; he is one of
our decidedly inferior men, and the chief features of
my small apartment are dirt, cobwebs and general
disorder. His children have been suffering from fever,
he tells me, and well they may, living in such an insanitary home."

After the fatigues of that week and the assaults of
mosquitoes, with disturbed nights, it was not remarkable that he should have to stay a week in the house
with fever—a very frequent concomitant of over-
exertion.

The evangelist at the first of these stations to be
visited has written a few reminiscences, which form an
interesting commentary on Mr. Pearse's own diary :

" In our part of the world there were twenty-one
churches of which the nearest, the place at which I was
living, was about twenty-two miles from the capital.

" The churches were rather far apart and the roads were
bad ; hills, valleys and streams were numerous and all
had to be crossed. In spite of all that, Mr. Pearse used
to visit us frequently, and he was always in good time.
There were three evangelists, and he used to visit us all.
Some of the churches joined together for their services,
but the smaller ones he liked to visit individually.

"The distance prevented his meeting us before eleven
a.m., just the time that one is feeling tired and done up,
but he put up with that. When he joined us at meals,
he always wanted us to prepare something quite simple ;

one of his favourite dishes consisted of vegetable marrow
leaves.   At one church he did not wish the people to
put themselves to the trouble of cooking a great feast,
so he said to the pastor : ' Just a little soft manioc is
what I like best.'   And although the people cooked
their feast, he began with the manioc and enjoyed that
most.

" The houses were not very clean, but if time allowed
he used to go with the evangelist and the pastor to some
of the nearer ones to encourage the people.   The people
would swarm into the room and conversation would
become general, the state of the church, whether prosperous or otherwise, would be discussed, and he would
make wise suggestions as to what should be done.   The
people were never afraid of speaking before him, and
we used to have delightful times.

" The progress of the kingdom of God was his great
desire.   He stirred up the evangelists and pastors to
do their best and tried to rouse the churches as well.
There were two churches that had to be rebuilt; times
were bad and the people did not know where to find
the means of finishing them. He helped them both, and
gave them a good deal, after which they worked with
a will and completed their task.   Sometimes when he
heard of a church being in any difficulty, he would write
an epistle to them to help them.

:" He always encouraged the people to buy books,
especially the Bible. He used to place a good many
Bibles with us for sale, so that the people would not
have the excuse of saying that they had no Bibles,
because they could not go so far as the capital to buy.
These Bibles were all very soon disposed of.

" Those who had boys he liked to encourage to send
them up to the capital, if they were scholarly ; some he

took into his own home and many of them did well, some obtaining their diploma as teachers and some becoming evangelists.

"When he was leaving for England he wrote to my wife and me, and asked: ' Are all the people in your care Christians ? ' and this roused us to work all the harder, so as to try and bring Christianity to everyone about us."

The work done in the boys' home exerted a great influence among the lads; the loving care exercised over them in all their concerns, combined with the example continually before them of Christian living, made an impression upon them. One of them alludes to that time when he says: "What Mr. and Mrs. Pearse did for those boys was beyond the power of words to express. They were truly grandparents to us. I always remember how Mr. Pearse used to read us the eighty-fourth Psalm every Sunday evening : ' How amiable are thy tabernacles, O Lord of hosts.' There was one of the boys who was very troublesome indeed. Mr. Pearse spoke to him just once ; no stripes, no anger but just a quiet talk and the boy left his presence weeping, conquered by love."

Before passing from this period, there is another visit to the district to be alluded to. There had been the usual journeyings, preaching, hospitality on the part of the natives, and description of the quantity of rice and pork served up in unappetizing abundance !

There were no less than five chapel-opening services during that week, of which he says : " To account for such a number you must remember that after the French had victoriously entered the capital, this was one of the districts in which the rebellion rose to its height and some of the chapels were burned or otherwise destroyed by the rebel bands. Hence nearly everywhere, the former chapels have had to be repaired and renovated, or else new ones have had to be built. It is a very bright feature connected with Protestant Christianity that, instead of giving way to despair, the people have risen to the occasion and set to work so heartily to provide themselves again with church accommodation. The churches were not infrequently crowded to excess.

"_Sunday_.—I was very feverish and unwell all night, and got up with a bad headache. Took an early cup of tea and started off for another village, where we had a _very_ enjoyable service. Really it was good to be there and it is matter for profound gratitude and joy that, so soon after war and rebellion, such a service could be held. The chapel is a simple, neat, clean building, and the order and behaviour of the congregation all that the most fastidious could desire. I was a little surprised when, after announcing a hymn, the pastor said : ' After the hymn, one sister will read the Scriptures, and another will lead in prayer.' How well that woman read ! She selected the sixtieth chapter of Isaiah and from beginning to end there was not a single mistake, and the tone and expression and emphasis were perfect. She is the mother of quite a young baby, which she brought to church with her, but committed to the kind care of another woman, while she read."

About this time Mr. and Mrs. Pearse were able to welcome one of their daughters, who, with her husband and child, had the happiness of residing near them in Antanànarìvo during the rest of their term of service. For the first time they were able to take into their arms a grandchild of their own, who, though not actually their first grandchild, was the first to be introduced to

them. Thus joys of another character entered their
lives and cheered them after the trials and difficulties
they had had so large a share of.

In due course the departments of work taken up as
locum tenens reverted to others, and Mr. Pearse became
free to give similar assistance to other brethren. The
school passed into the hands of Mr. Thorne, and the
Isòtry district, of Mr. Baron, but the district of Anàlakèly
became vacant by the departure of Mr. Sibree, and to the
mutual pleasure of both himself and the congregations,
Mr. Pearse was again asked to superintend them. Bible-
classes in the country were again part of his responsibility, and he was already engaged in preparing commentaries on the Epistles to the Philippians and the
Thessalonians. His charge of the church at Anàlakèly
coincided with a very delicate period of its history
with regard to the pastorate, as the old pastor was
paralyzed and the church was suffering for want of a
suitable native at its head, only the choice was found to
be very difficult. His leading at that particular time
was wise and helpful, and was useful in bringing the
church to a sense of union. On his return to Madagascar,
after furlough, in October, 1901, Mr. Sibree wrote :
" It is a matter for great satisfaction to see how
prosperous our mother-church at Anàlakèly is, and also
what progress has been made during our absence among
the village congregations. The testimony of all who
come to see us is that advance is being everywhere made
and the prospects of Christian work seem most cheering
and hopeful. We feel sure that much of this (as regards
our own district) is owing to the very earnest and faithful
labour of our dear friends, Mr. and Mrs. Pearse. They
have both been unwearied in carrying on the work, in
Bible-classes, Sunday School and Christian Endeavour

efforts, and, on Mr. Pearse's part, of constant preaching
and pastoral work."

He was also engaged for part of this time in teaching
at the L.M.S. College, which has now become the
United Theological College, under that mission and that
of the Friends. Medical work no longer entered into
Mr. Pearse's programme ; but he retained a great
interest in what was going on at the Medical Mission.

Two further allusions must be made to events in
Antsihànaka, with a view of rounding off the story
of that province. The diary records : "Monsieur
Mondain of the Mission Protestante Française, has just
returned from a flying visit to Ambàtondrazàka and
Imèrimandròso, paid at the request of the committee of
the native Congregational Union, which has recently
sent a second evangelist to the province. The report he
brings back is very encouraging, and light is evidently
again breaking upon that part of Madagascar. Yesterday it was my pleasure to despatch a hundred Bibles
to Ambàtondrazàka, for the purchase of which there
is arising an eager demand. During the unfortunate
rebellion nearly every copy of the scriptures in the
district was destroyed."

The other incident was the recording, in a letter
dated 5th October, 1899, of an act of reparation, which
gave him great pleasure and spoke well for those in
power who brought it about. The letter says :—

"Last year I had to chronicle the unjust manner in
which Rajàofèra had been treated, and to tell of his
peremptory expulsion from the Antsihànaka territory,
after having served there faithfully as an evangelist for
the long period of twenty years. His association with
us was known to be the only reason for this unjust and
cruel treatment.

" It is with very great pleasure that I write to-day to inform you that justice is now being shown to this most worthy man, and, before this letter is away from here, Rajàofèra and his wife will be on their way back to Imèrimandròso. Every charge against him is withdrawn ; the medal which was voted to him by the French Home Government, but which the officer in charge at Ambàtondrazàka refused to bestow, is to be given to him, and his worthiness to receive it fully acknowledged, and he is to be reinstated into the position which he occupied before his expulsion, or to be placed in one of greater importance and influence.

"From Rajàofèra's own statement to me, the following appear to be the chief facts :

" Madame Pennequin, the wife of the Governor-General, holds receptions for the natives every Tuesday afternoon, and through the native interpreter, Rajàofèra was induced to visit Madame, on the 26th ult. The conversation turned on Antsihànaka, and Rajàofèra's long connection with that part of the island. Madame, and the French officer present in attendance on her, manifested great interest, and drew from Rajàofèra some of the particulars of the circumstances under which he had to leave Antsihànaka. Then and there sympathy with Rajàofèra and his wife was expressed, and the matter was taken up without delay. Rajàofèra was asked if he wished to go back, and upon his replying in the affirmative, he was encouraged to hope that his wish would be fulfilled. Four days after, i.e., last Saturday morning, in answer to a call which he received, Rajàofèra was again at the General's quarters, when the good news I have stated above was announced to him, and official letters were handed to him introducing him to the chief officer at

Ambàtondrazàka, as a native who has been unjustly treated in the past, and to whom all honour is to be shown, and in whom the fullest confidence is to be placed in the future.

" This is good news indeed. Through the door thus opened, it may be that other evangelists, and (if they can be sent) missionaries, may enter and resume work among the Sihànaka."

A quotation from Dr. Maclaren pleased him very much : " If your business is to keep the door, you will not be leaving, but abiding in the secret place of the Most High if you get up from your knees in the middle of your prayer and go down to open it. The smallest, commonest acts of daily life are truer worship than is rapt or solitary communion or united prayer, if the latter can only be secured at the neglect of the former. Better be in the lowly parts of the house, attending to the humblest duties, than to be in the upper chambers, uniting with the saints in supplication, and leaving tasks unperformed."

During the latter part of this term of service Mr. Pearse suffered much from a very debilitating ailment and a good deal of his work had to be accomplished under considerable difficulties. The time of furlough was therefore welcomed, and preparations were made for leaving the island in April, 1902. The return of friends from their furloughs released him, so that it was chiefly the endeavour to complete his literary work, as well as the exigences of the season, that detained him. During the last few weeks there were many farewell gatherings of interest, as well as visits paid by him to most of the institutions of the capital, so that he might have some idea of their progress. Thus boys' schools and girls' schools were visited, services attended at many churches both in town and country, where the entries in the diary record with pleasure such impressions as " Chapel quite full. Behaviour of all most becoming and devout." A visit is recorded to General Gallieni, who was " most gracious and gave an introduction to his officers at the various ' postes ' *en route* to Tamatàve." The six-monthly meeting of the Congregational Union, an institution with which he had been connected from its very commencement ; a meeting of the students of the college, past and present ; and finally, a large meeting, called specially to bid farewell to the three families returning, were among the final gatherings attended. At the latter he, and Mr. Briggs, who, it will be remembered, left England in the same ship with him nearly forty years before, and also Monsieur Ducommun, all spoke, and much feeling was aroused by the announcement that he, at any rate, scarcely expected to return to Madagascar again.

Finally they were accompanied from the town by a large number of friends, as they departed this time not in palanquins, but in rickshas, in which the first part of the journey was accomplished. Good roads made this possible, and on approaching the coast, they were able to experience, what in their wildest dreams would never have entered their imaginations a few years previously, a railway journey in Madagascar.

CHAPTER XV

Material Progress

Soon after arriving in England in 1902, the following interesting account, by Mr. Pearse, of the changes in the island which resulted from the French occupation, appeared in the *Christian World* :

" All who have had the opportunity of observing what has taken place during the past six years will acknowledge that most beneficial changes have been in-troduced since the tricolour of France was raised on the Palace of the Hova sovereigns, and none who are acquainted with the present condition of things will deny that great and rapid progress has taken place.

" One of the first objects upon which the French concentrated their energies was that of improving the condition of the roads. No roads, in the civilized sense of that term, existed in Madagascar at the date of the occupation. Even in the capital the thoroughfares were rough and wretched in the extreme, and were a combined footpath, dust-bin, dung-hill and sewer ; during the rainy season the heavy tropical showers dug gullies many feet deep in the main streets. The routes to the country towns and villages and to the distant parts of the island were along the narrow tracks worn by native pedestrians from time immemorial. Many were so narrow that they could only be followed by walking in single file. Bogs and sloughs were serious obstacles, streams and rivers had to be forded or swum, dense brushwood and intertwining creepers had to be fought and fallen tree-trunks vaulted over or crawled under.

" To-day it is as though an enchanter's wand had been waved over Antanànarìvo and some parts of the country. Broad, smooth thoroughfares of easy gradients now traverse the city in various directions, and make most parts of it easy of access. Stone water-courses bound these thoroughfares on either side and carry the heavy rains to underground sewers, along which it is conveyed to the rice-fields. Refuse and rubbish no longer, to the same extent as formerly, offend either the sense of sight or smell, or render the condition insanitary; scavengers are on duty every day, and keep the streets as clean as those in Paris itself. Nor has the ornamental been forgotten or neglected. Trees have been planted along many of the avenues and in other favourable situations, and the two large open spaces, known formerly as Andohàlo and Anjomà, have undergone a wonderful and beautiful transformation. Here in days past were found the unsightly bazaars in which native traders displayed every description of wares upon the ground or on rude wooden stalls, while they themselves lounged or squatted lazily by the side waiting for customers ; here also oxen and sheep were slaughtered daily in the sight of passers-by, and under the keen and anticipating gaze of a crowd of lean and hungry dogs. These spots have been converted into what are now known as 'La Place Jean-Laborde ' and ' La Place Colbert,' in which choice shrubs and flowers flourish and a military band plays twice a week. Excellent roads also radiate from Antanànarìvo into the suburbs and outlying districts, while broad highways have taken the place of the previous narrow and miry tracks, to the distant parts of

the island. The road which connects Antanànarìvo
with the east coast is a marvellous piece of engineering.
Automobiles, bicycles, ox-waggons, hand-carts and
jinrickshas may all be seen upon it. The swamps have
been drained, valleys have been filled in, ferry-boats
have been provided for the conveyance of vehicles and
goods over the larger rivers, while bridges span the
smaller ones ; the whole route has, in fact, been brought
into a condition which allows it to be placed in highly
favourable comparison with many of the main roads in
Europe.

"Another very great public benefit introduced by the
French has been the establishment of an excellent
postal service. Life in the interior of Madagascar during
the reign of the Hova sovereigns was, to a great extent,
a condition of isolation from the civilized world outside.
By hiring your own messenger, letters could, indeed, be
taken to Tamatàve, whence they were sooner or later
conveyed over the sea by any merchant sailing-vessel
which happened to call, and in the same way, letters
and newspapers were received from correspondents
and friends ; but, until within a few years of the occupation, all was irregular and uncertain and slow at
the best. Madagascar is now included in the Postal
Union and, under subsidy from the French Government,
there is a bi-monthly mail service. After being landed
from the steamer the mail-bags for the interior are
despatched either by relays of native runners, or, more
recently, in carts drawn by mules, the animals being
changed frequently *en route*, and the mails thus reach the
capital with an expedition which, until the railroad now
in course of construction is completed, it will surely be
impossible to exceed. The postage rate for letters to
any part of the interior is three half-pence for the half-

ounce. Periodicals, published in the Island, are carried for the infinitesimal charge of one centime for fifty grammes (about 1½ oz.)! This is worth the notice of the Postmaster-General in England, as an example of interest in the public welfare. An internal parcels post is also fully developed.

"The telegraph and telephone services are fast approaching perfection. In walking through the city not very long ago, I counted more than thirty wires connected with these services suspended overhead. Telegraph messages can be sent throughout the Island at the rate of one penny per word, with a minimum charge of one franc for a single telegram. A submarine cable has been laid across the Mozambique Channel, which connects Madagascar with the whole of the outside civilized world. We not only get 'Reuter's' messages by telegram from the coast, but all the most important items of foreign news are received by cable-gram by the Governor-General, and are posted up in prominent centres for the information of the public. Considerable sums have been voted in the French Chamber for the establishment of hospitals and dispensaries in the colony. These philanthropic efforts on the part of the Government impress an old resident very emphatically, inasmuch as they stand in striking contrast to the meagre action taken by the authorities in all such matters during the old *régime*. With the exception of a single small hospital, opened during the reign of Rànavàlona II., the only public efforts put forth for the benefit of the sick, and for the relief of the suffering, before the time of the occupation of Madagascar by France, were those of the various missions, which did quietly and unostentatiously an amount of good to which it is impossible to refer except in terms of the highest praise. After the union, France immediately commenced to show that she recognized that the main responsibility of caring for the sick and suffering rested upon her, and that the duty of using means to secure the physical well-being of the members of her adopted large family ought not to be relegated to others. In addition to the military hospitals and infirmaries now found here, in a prominent position on the south-east ridge of the hill upon which Antanànarîvo is built, a well-equipped hospital has been established which is open to any Malagasy who applies for admission. The patients are treated by French physicians and surgeons, assisted by educated natives. Similar but smaller institutions have been established in the country districts, and also in some of the remote parts of the island. The number of such hospitals is being gradually increased, and to-day, while I am writing these lines, General Gallieni is away from the city opening one recently completed, in the centre of the important district of Arivonimamo, in the west. In connection with the civil hospital referred to above, a school of medicine, for the education and training of native doctors, was star ted as soon as it was practicable to do so after the occupation, thus continuing the work of teaching carried on for many years by the medical missionaries. Some of the students have already completed the curriculum and have received their diplomas, and are practising in various places with success. Passing through a village last Saturday morning, my attention was attracted by the number of persons I observed crowding within a building, the large door of which was open to the public thoroughfare. On reading the notice displayed above the door, I found that the building was being used as a dispensary, where sick people could receive advice and be supplied

with medicine gratis. Similar dispensaries have been
opened and are worked and supported by the Government in a good many of the populous centres of the
Province of Imèrina.

" Schools have been established in which a general
elementary education is given to both sexes of the rising
generation of Malagasy. Attendance has not yet been
made compulsory, but at many it is large and regular.
In Antanànarìvo there is a normal school,where the course
of study includes instruction—by European teachers
—in history, mathematics, political economy, science,
drawing and other subjects. Supported by the Government, there is also ' L'École Professionelle ' for native
artisans, and here, under European superintendence,
various arts are taught, which include tanning, carpentry,
pottery, smith's work, weaving and horology. Courts
of law, after the European model, have been brought
into existence, where justice is administered equally
to all classes of the community. Bribery and extortion,
formerly practised to an unlimited extent, and which so
frightfully disgraced many of the highest officials during
the Hova administration, are strictly prohibited ; and
if any of the native employees in the public service are
discovered to be still carrying on such unworthy practices,
they are forthwith removed from their positions, and
severely fined or imprisoned. Order is maintained in
the capital by an organized body of native police. The
markets have been subjected to very sweeping reforms.
Adulterated articles, diseased meat, and unripe and
unsound fruits are proscribed. Weights and measures
are inspected and must conform to the Government
standards. Purchasers in the markets and stores no
longer require the small scales and the accompanying
weights which were formerly essential for the comple-

tion of every trading transaction, for the copper and silver coins of the Republic have taken the place of the cut-money which used to be the only currency. Slavery is no longer an institution in the land ; every man, woman and child is free. And not only this, but the compulsory and unpaid Government service which so fearfully oppressed the Malagasy under their own rulers, has been, more recently, also abolished by France, and all service and labour required by the Government is paid for in an honest manner and according to a liberal rate. Under the petty local administration in the country districts, a form of ' prestation ' (Commune business, in the French meaning of that term) is, I fear, still made somewhat oppressive. Religion receives no official patronage, but, at the same time, it is neither discouraged nor persecuted. Absolute religious liberty is granted to all. The sale of intoxicants to the natives is not yet, I regret to say, prohibited or controlled by any laws. By his personal habits, both in private and on all public occasions, General Gallieni exercises an influence decidedly in favour of temperance. Juvenile smoking is strictly forbidden.

" It is gratifying to be able thus to bear honest testimony to the many praiseworthy efforts being made by France to promote the social well-being of the Malagasy, and to advance what is right and wise and good among them. These efforts will, it may be hoped, be crowned with success, and cause Madagascar, ere long, to occupy a position of honour in the ranks of the civilized and educated nations of the world."

CHAPTER XVI

Closing Years

1902 to 1911.

THE voyage to England was a trying one, partly on account of the enfeebled state of Mr. Pearse's own health, and partly owing to the great anxiety which he and the rest of the party had over the very serious illness of a fellow-missionary: Through the care and attention bestowed upon this lady, her life was spared, so that her friends were fully rewarded for all they had attempted to do for her.

On arrival, Mr. Pearse lost no time in placing himself in the surgeon's hands and, after the necessary operation, he soon began to regain something of his usual vigour. The time of furlough was spent quietly, and there were many opportunities of meeting with various members of his family and with his children, that brought much joy and delight. It was not possible to engage in much deputation work, but he had the pleasure of knowing that his efforts were the means of doing good to some. The Rev. A. N. Johnson wrote to tell him, some years later, of one such incident : " I was informed that you were at a certain church and very greatly delighted all who heard you. Amongst the audience was a man who had hardly ever been in a chapel before ; he was greatly interested in your address, and was led by it (so his wife

said) to think seriously on higher things. He has now
come out definitely as a follower of Christ."

Much earnest thought was given to the future. Mr.
Pearse was in his sixty-sixth year and, after a life of
great activity and much strain, was feeling the need of
rest. At the same time, his constitution was still strong,
he did not take kindly to English life, and especially to
English weather, and he received constant reminders
from Madagascar that there was congenial work there
that he might still do, under congenial conditions. This
not unnaturally led him to seriously consider the question
of return for another term of service, and the decision
was eventually taken in favour of so doing. His health,
however, proved to be not as sufficiently restored as he
and others had hoped, and on arrival in Madagascar,
in October, 1903, he felt that, though physically strong,
he was unequal to what he had to do. The opportunities
for work were many, and he made full use of them, and
his ministry was received with great appreciation. There
was not, however, quite the same regular employment
that he had always been accustomed to, as he went out,
not to take up a district, but to render help as it might be
needed, and this in itself proved irksome to his orderly
mind. He was able to continue his Bible classes with
very gratifying results, to write for the press, revising
his commentary on 1 Corinthians, as well as doing other
literary work, to visit the hospital, where he read and
talked with the patients with infinite acceptance, and
to undertake preaching engagements, for which he was
as much sought after as ever. His ministrations were
received with unabated delight.

He wrote on his return to Madagascar : " From the
missionary standpoint, my impressions are decidedly
favourable. There have been advance and improve-

ment since we left in the spring of 1902.   The attendance at the services which I have taken part in has been excellent, and the reverent behaviour and attention of the congregations is very striking.   Last Thursday afternoon, Mrs. Pearse and I were at a church, where the young Christian Endeavourers in connection with some of the churches in Antanànarìvo and the suburbs, had arranged to hold a united service.   I estimated the attendance at about 800.   One old woman (probably eighty years of age) who was present asked to be allowed to say a few words.   The permission was, of course, granted, and in a very pathetic manner she contrasted the favourable conditions under which Christianity can now be followed, with the cruel persecutions which she and others had to endure in her early days."

As time went on, the strain on Mr. Pearse's health aroused alarm, so that it appeared imperative that he should finally terminate his connection with Madagascar, and this, though a severe trial, was bravely faced. There was no formal farewell.   His work was just relinquished; he preached for the last time with his usual power and ease, so that some of us who were present wondered at the irony that removed such a force from our midst ; there was no sign, in the quality of the work done, of any failure of power, and, apart from the particular condition of health which indicated otherwise, he might have still hoped for a long continuance of the life on the mission field which had grown so dear to him. Followed by the love and devotion of thousands in Madagascar, Mr. and Mrs. Pearse left Antanànarìvo in September, 1904.

On arrival in England, they settled first, for a few months, at St. Ives, Hunts, and later at Mortimer, near Reading, where they had the joy of being near one

of their married daughters.   For many years Mr. Pearse
had made very frequent allusions, in his letters home, to
the " three-roomed cottage " in which the " evening of
ife " was to be spent.   At length the time for its
occupation arrived, and the residence proved to be one
of somewhat more ambitious proportions, with a nice
garden attached, where he might follow the one hobby
he had indulged in ; and the immediate neighbourhood, with its heaths and pinewoods, was exceedingly
charming.

Here opportunities came for exercising his genial
and gracious influence and, at times, for some public
work.   A young French lady wrote of " the depth in his
eyes and the tender dignity of his life," which had been
instrumental in influencing her.   She added, in speaking
of a short stay under his roof, that it " lighted the path
of life for me with a light which ever gleamed henceforth."

In 1908 the great missionary exhibition of the London
Missionary Society, the " Orient," was held in London.
The services of all available missionaries were requisi-
tioned, and Mr. Pearse took his place in working there.
His efforts were warmly appreciated and his talks on
mission work and experiences were greatly enjoyed by
very many.   The opportunity of again doing some
active missionary work, though it was physically very
exhausting to him, proved to be an excellent tonic,
and, from this time onward, his general health improved
greatly, he became more reconciled to the break with
Madagascar, and he settled down, with greater satisfaction, to his garden, his correspondence and his
reading.   His letters had a note of gaiety and well-being,
which made them a treat for the recipients.

He found more pleasure in public engagements, took

the chair at meetings in his own village, preached more frequently in the neighbourhood and took several services for the London Missionary Society, giving valued assistance in one place and another and leading his hearers to increased interest in and sympathy with missionary efforts in Madagascar. He enjoyed visiting the cottagers and helping them in their trials, and was much used, as previously in Madagascar, to their strengthening and uplifting. A pretty insight into his life at the time is furnished by a letter written to one of his sons : " I saw him but once, yet often remember the pleasant time we spent together. The children were at Mortimer, and I went there to see them. Your father met me at the station, and as strangers we introduced ourselves and soon became on easy and friendly terms. His quiet, serious, yet informing manner pleased me and I felt that with a better acquaintance we should become friends. In the afternoon, he drove me through the pinewoods for many miles, and through the pleasant villages of an English rural country that was new to me, and we talked of many things and passing objects. The children were with us, restless, noisy and in exuberant spirits, on the opposite seat, all of which he took quietly and kindly, answering their questions and encouraging them in their fun, as age does or should do with the little ones. It was an October day, yet warm and genial as summer, a cloudless sky and a sunlight that broke through every crevice, spangling the floor of the pinewoods and lighting the highways into whiteness, and its influence and spell were upon us all."

Towards the close of 1910 he and Mrs. Pearse visited several of the members of their family. He was able to undertake some public engagements and thus the visit was memorable to others besides his own immediate circle. An influence of deep yet radiant peacefulness spread from him. Unconsciously perhaps, he was led to put in order many little matters that claimed attention.

Finally, there came Christmas, spent, as usual, with gladness and joy at the home of one of their daughters.

On the first Sunday of 1911, though somewhat indisposed, he occupied the pulpit at the little church at Mortimer West and gave a strong and cheery message for the New Year from the text : Phil. iii. 13 and 14.

Circumstances necessitated his walking out again for the evening service, and in his anxiety not to be late, he ran some part of the three miles of road between his home and the chapel. He conducted the service, but the effort had so exhausted the heart that his condition soon became serious, and before the end of that week, even urgent.

His daughter, Dr. Margaret Alden, has contributed the following recollections of his last illness : " During the second week he seemed less well and attacks of severe breathlessness added a more serious aspect to his condition. It was evident that heart weakness had set in, and the shadow of a fear arose that life might even be threatened. But watchful care, aided by a loyal response on his part to the orders of his doctors, soon brought an improvement which rejoiced the hearts of all. The patience of this strong man stricken down was a moving lesson to those about him. No injunction was too small for him to carry out and restrictions were accepted without murmuring. During these early days of weakness he asked that a favourite book might be read to him ' The Kingship of Self-Control.' He had no need of its teaching, for he had verily attained to this kingship.

" Throughout the first fortnight of January a patient, noble fight was fought. Ultimately the exhausting breathlessness lessened, and hope cheered all hearts. But soon the heart condition failed to respond to treatment and progressive weakness set in and hope had to be abandoned. The spirit maintained its supremacy, and we watched with heart-broken admiration this warrior waging his last warfare with the enemy that must, in the end, prove victorious.

" He spoke little, for all his strength was needed to carry on the daily conflict. But one night his soul uttered its yearnings aloud as verse after verse from the Psalms escaped him in breathless whispers. ' Bless the Lord, O my soul, who forgiveth all thy iniquities, who healeth all thy diseases, who crowneth thee with loving-kindness and tender mercies.' ' He that dwelleth in the secret place of the Most High shall abide under the shadow of the Almighty.' ' He shall cover thee with His feathers, and under His wings shalt thou trust. His truth shall be thy shield and buckler.' As the month of January drew to a close, each day made it more sadly certain that the last farewells must soon be said. His feet were entering the valley of the shadow, which leads to the city of God and the palace of the King. Very early in the morning of February 3rd the release came. As the last short breaths were drawn, the expression of suffering faded away, a radiance of joy overspread the beloved face and we knew that an entrance had been ministered unto him abundantly into the everlasting kingdom.

*   *   *   *   *

" It is not easy to realize that this strenuous life is over. Over, merely from the standpoint of the daily going in and out amongst us, but living yet in its in-

fluence in the hearts and lives of men and women. The
soldier of the Lord has laid down his sword, the man of
effort has faced his last earthly task. As he lay in the
silent chamber of death his whole bearing breathed
forth the unmistakable message : ' I have fought a
good fight,' and the one reply bursting from our hearts
with our tears, was : ' Well done, good and faithful
servant, enter thou into the joy of thy Lord.' "

In due course he was borne to his rest in the lovely
calm of the beautiful little churchyard of St. Mary's,
Mortimer, where he had desired to be. His Malagasy
hymn-book was laid on his breast, and amid a profusion
of white flowers, chrysanthemums and snowdrops, the
mortal was committed to the dust.

An old man wept as the *cortége* passed, saying, " I
shall never have such a friend again."

The Rev. Canon C. Lovett Cameron, the Vicar of the
parish, had wished to be present himself to conduct
the funeral service, but serious illness prevented him, and
his place was taken by the Rev. F. Taylor, M.A.

When the news reached Madagascar, there were
innumerable marks of respect and sorrow. From the
churches at Antanànarìvo, in the district of Anàlakèly,
in the provinces of Antsihànaka and Bètsilèo and from
many an isolated friend in other parts of the island came
tributes of affection. Every day for weeks the natives
came to call on his daughter and son-in-law to offer
condolence and to say what Mr. Pearse had been to
them and how they had loved him. As the custom is,
offerings of money were made, and these sums have
been used by the family in putting up a brass tablet
in the church at Anàlakèly to record the labours of over
forty years for Madagascar, finishing up with the
text so often quoted : " Blessed are the dead that die

in the Lord ; they rest from their labours and their
works do follow them."

In Ambàtondrazàka, an old man was told that Mr.
Pearse was gone, and forthwith commenced to clap his
hands. The evangelist, who had given the news,
thought he had been misunderstood, but the old man
invited him in and then he knelt down and poured
forth his thanksgivings for the life lived and the work
done ; and then he explained. He could not help
clapping, he said, for his friend had gone before, and
now was awaiting him on the other side, to welcome him.

Impressive memorial services were held in several
places. At Anàlakèly, members of other missionary
societies joined in their testimony and brief appreciations
were offered by the Rev. J. Sibree, a friend of nearly
half a century, and several natives. A choice little
address was given by Andriamifìdy, now pastor of one
of the memorial churches, formerly minister for foreign
affairs in the native cabinet.

Another service was held in the district at Ambà-
tofòtsy, and again Mr. Sibree gave his testimony, and
several natives who had worked with Mr. Pearse as
evangelists and teachers, one, even in Antsihànaka,
gave interesting reminiscences, some of which have
been already quoted. Mention was made of what
Mr. Pearse had done for them, the churches he had helped
them to erect, the windows he had given, the bell he had
helped them to procure, but always the great feature
of his work was brought out : his ardent love for the
Malagasy, which led him to engage in such a variety
of labour in order to influence them for Christ. A third
meeting was held at a place, Ambòhitràrahàba, where
one of the martyrs had lived and where Mr. Pearse had
spent some happy holidays as well as done much pains-

taking work. At Fìanàrantsòa, a united meeting of the missions was held in commemoration of his seventeen years of service, and honour was done to his memory by the unanimity of the gathering.

By many writing at the time, various characteristics were emphasized and the beauty and power of his life were alluded to. The testimony of these pages will explain them all. The guiding power was the Spirit of Christ. Devotion to Him and His service animated his words and actions. Built on the natural traits of thoroughness, perseverance and order, were the graces of sympathy, persuasiveness and faithfulness. Combined with these were his high ability as a Malagasy scholar, as a preacher and writer, as a doctor and man of affairs. He was able to turn his hands to almost every kind of work and in all that he did there was the mark of distinction. A most marked feature was his unswerving and conscientious devotion to duty. He was able in a wonderful manner to rise to emergencies, and his spoken utterances on great occasions were admirable. One wrote of the " inspiration of his message, confirmed by his consecrated life " ; another, of the " kind friend and beautiful helper of all who needed " ; another of " his entirely unselfish and active life " ; a fourth, of his " strong, kindly personality." One spoke of him as " so thoughtful and gracious " ; and another, of the " Master's faithful and loyal-hearted servant " ; and so, with a recognition of the many-sided elements of his character, they paid him their tribute. And what others recognized from their knowledge of him in a wider circle, was not belied by the more intimate knowledge of his own. Their tribute is the same, but with super-added veneration and sweetness. And those who saw most of him were the ones who knew best. He was

preaching once, on the subject: " A man of God," based
on the prophet Elijah, and he remarked: " If you want
to know of me, whether I am a man of God or not, go
to Inèny Ramànandrày and Ingàhy Ràinikàla (his
old servants, who were with him over thirty years),
and they will tell you all about my life, for they see
it." And so it was.

His life was summed up in a beautiful resolution
passed by the Southern Committee of the Board of the
London Missionary Society :—

" That in recording the death of the Rev. Joseph
Pearse, and in tendering to Mrs. Pearse and family
their heartfelt sympathy, the Directors claim the
privilege of paying affectionate tribute to the distinguished labours of their friend in Madagascar, and of
expressing their high esteem for a saintly life of bound-
less love for God and the Malagasy. In that spirit
of love he devoted himself without sparing to the
work of evangelist, teacher, healer, and with great
courage, gentle of spirit though he was, he faced the
difficulties and dangers of the pioneer. At his desk,
as a Bible commentator, in the pulpit, as an eloquent
preacher, with exceptional grasp of the native language,
and on the field among semi-barbarians he was a man
of power because he was a man of prayer. To the last
his thoughts went out in affection to the colleagues
and Malagasy among whom he had laboured with so
much joy and profit."

CHAPTER XVII

Testimony of Fellow-Workers

FROM various fellow-workers in Madagascar reminiscences have been received, which further indicate the affection and esteem in which Mr. Pearse was held. Each of the following presents its own special points of interest.

The first is from his friend of nearly fifty years standing, the Rev. James Sibree, F.R.G.S., the senior missionary of the London Missionary Society in Madagascar; the next from Miss Clark, of the Friends' Foreign Mission Association, daughter of the late Mr. Henry E. Clark, who was for so long a missionary of the latter society; following that is a short appreciation of Mr. Pearse's preaching and writing, from the pen of the Rev. W. E. Cousins, M.A., one of the first missionaries to enter Madagascar after the persecution; and finally, there is a tribute from the Rev. H. T. Johnson, who was associated with him in work in the Bètsilèo Province for nearly twenty years.

Mr. Sibree writes : " I had the privilege of knowing, pretty intimately, Mr. Pearse ever since his and my first arrival in Madagascar, now more than forty-eight years ago. He and his first wife arrived in Antanànarîvo only six days before I got up here myself (October 13th, 1863) and as the small house they occupied was just below the place where I lived, I saw them very frequently. They were content to live in a very humble little native dwelling, a wooden structure, devoid of most of the comforts which, in later years, have been considered essential for the missionary's home.

"Although Mr. Pearse became eventually one of the most accomplished speakers and writers in the Malagasy language, he was not very quick in acquiring the speech of the people, and it was about a year before he began to preach in the language. This was, however, partly due to the anxiety caused by the illness and death of his wife, who was not here many months before signs of consumption developed. After her death, Mr. Pearse returned, sad and solitary, to the capital and applied himself with fresh energy to his work. The departure of the Rev. J. Duffus for England left vacant the position of missionary at the church of Anàlakèly, and Mr. Pearse took charge of the congregation there, together with its half-dozen or so country churches. After gaining a good knowledge of the language, he soon became a very able and earnest preacher and speaker, and his sententious and weighty delivery, his intimate knowledge of native habits and ways of thinking, and his genial manner, made him before long a favourite among the Malagasy churches, and he was much sought after for special services.

"The desirability of a new building for the Anàlakèly congregation soon engaged his attention, and he did much, in conjunction with Mr. Cameron, who attended that church, to stir up the people to build a more suitable structure for divine worship. I well remember the day of the opening and the admiration of all at the new building, which was an immense advance upon any ecclesiastical structure which had, up to then, been seen in Madagascar.

"Mr. Pearse did very much in regular Bible-class instruction and so raised up an intelligent body of Christian people and preachers, not only in the Anàlakèly church, but in the country congregations dependent on it.

"Mr. Pearse was able to follow closely in the steps of the apostle Paul, in becoming ' all things to all men.' He had a good knowledge of human nature, and was most tactful in dealing with different kinds of people. It used to be said that he could make a better bargain for work and materials and for workpeople than the Malagasy themselves, and this was because he had such an intimate acquaintance with their ways. He made them feel that they were doing themselves a pleasure in agreeing to his proposals. If he had to refuse a request, it was done in such a way that it pleased the asker more even than the granting would have done in the case of most other missionaries. I well remember hearing his reply to someone who came asking for quinine. Mr. Pearse, after a few pleasant words of sympathy and kind enquiries, said: ' I certainly have some quinine, my friend, but there is not enough to divide between us.' His was, eminently, ' the art of putting things.' The man went off quite contented, invoking a blessing on his missionary !

"Mr. Pearse had the happiness of making a second marriage in about two years after his arrival in Madagascar. Mrs. Pearse was the faithful companion and helper of her husband in all his work for forty-five years, and her children have risen up to fill honourable positions in life, in various ways, both at home and abroad.

"After his furlough he might have gone back to the pleasant house he had built for himself in the capital, and to the prosperous church he had so largely helped to instruct, but he felt deeply the needs of the less enlightened parts of Madagascar for missionary teaching, and so he offered to commence, on his return, a mission in the province of Antsihànaka. His unwearied service for the good of the people made a way to reach the hearts of many, and whatever progress there is now in Antsihànaka, is largely due to the good foundation laid there by Mr. and Mrs. Pearse. He had, during his furlough, given some time to the study of medicine and simple surgery, so that in a region without doctors he might ' heal the sick ' as well as ' preach the gospel ' to them. He became well-known among the Sihànaka as a healer and helper of the sick, and the story of one of his cures, the poor deserted and half-dead ' Lazarus,' has often been told. His experiences, together with much about his medical work, are described in a paper Mr. Pearse contributed to the *Antanànarìvo Annual* (No. viii., 1884 ; pp. 318-334). This paper, which is pervaded by a quiet humour, as well as pathos, forms an interesting chapter of missionary experience, well worthy a place side by side with chapters written by John Williams or Robert Moffat.

" There was, in 1881, urgent need for the help of an experienced missionary in the southern district of Bètsilèo. He felt constrained therefore to comply with the directors' wishes that he should remove to Fìanàrantsòa and become the senior missionary of that mission. Here he soon became recognized as the leader of the work, and here again his various gifts as preacher, teacher, writer, builder and doctor had free scope for their exercise.

" I shall never forget the impression he made upon me, as well as upon all his hearers, in an address he gave to a crowded meeting of the Congregational Union

of the Bètsilèo churches, at their annual gathering in
June, 1888. This was on : ' The service acceptable to
the Lord,' and in this he gave a masterly series of
illustrations, taken from things very familiar to the
Malagasy, such as gold, silk, cattle, etc., showing how
they came from sources mixed with much that
was low and unsightly but yet capable of being purified
and fitted for the highest service. This he applied
to the people themselves, showing how, although
impure, evil and degraded as they were by nature, the
gospel could and does raise them to be Christ's servants,
' vessels fit for the Master's use.' It was wonderfully
telling ; and as he described their cattle, being ill and
needing care, sometimes dying, there was quite a groan
went up from the assembly, people to whom their cattle
are their chief wealth, and on which a great proportion
of their time and care is spent.   One felt that he
had a wonderful gift of adapting his preaching to the
intelligence of his hearers ; no wonder that ' the common
people heard him gladly.'

   "Mr. Pearse had, hardly less, a gift in Bible-class
teaching. The substance of much of such teaching he
put in a permanent form in his most useful commentaries on several of the Epistles, and to his pen, Malagasy
literature owes a lasting debt of gratitude for these.
Many of his sermons were also printed and read with
delight by Malagasy preachers ; and probably were
frequently reproduced by them in their own pulpits.

   " Mr. Pearse's gifts as a versatile workman and builder
were soon put into service in Bètsilèo.   It was a pleasure
to me to help him by sending him a complete set of
drawings for the building of his church at Fìanàrantsòa.
This was carried out in a thoroughly substantial manner,
through his unremitting personal attention.

"Mr. Pearse's fame as a doctor increased during his residence in Bètsilèo. He became a very skilful physician, as well as a surgeon, and his help was sought for far and wide. The Malagasy had unbounded faith in his skill, and his help was often asked for by European traders and others on the coast, and although the journey to the southern ports was a difficult and fatiguing one, he did not hesitate to undertake it, when necessary, to attend to those who were in imminent danger. He was truly revered and loved by numbers who had benefited by his patient and self-denying care.

"It is a delight to me to remember that our friendship for forty-seven years was unbroken by a single cross word. Never did a mission have a more faithful worker, never have the Malagasy had a more loving missionary and teacher. As an able and earnest preacher of the gospel, as a most acceptable Bible-class teacher, as an instructive and helpful writer, as a skilful and beloved physician, as a true and staunch friend and fellow-worker the honoured and loved name of Joseph Pearse will long be remembered in Madagascar."

Miss Clark writes: "Mr. Pearse was an old friend and fellow-worker of my dear father, and their common love for the Malagasy, and desire to win them for Christ, united them very closely. For myself, I must always remember with gratitude the great kindness shown me by both Mr. and Mrs. Pearse when they were living at 'Mangarivotra,' Faravohitra, not far from the Friends' girls' school, where my work then lay. As I was alone there at that time, except for my family of native girls, I had a standing invitation to 'look in' at 'Mangarivotra' whenever passing, and was sure to meet with a hearty welcome whenever I did so, whilst much sympathetic interest in my work was always expressed. On

one occasion Mr. Pearse had preached at the chapel which
the girls and I attended that Sunday morning, and
hearing me say that the girls frequently wrote out in
the evening what they could remember of the morning's
sermon, he most kindly promised to give a prize for the
best paper that day, and I well remember how interested
he was in the girls' productions (feeble as some of them
were !) and how pleased with the one that both he and
I pronounced the best.

" Mr. Pearse's earnest and impressive manner when
speaking or preaching must be recalled by many.
One hymn in the Malagasy hymn-book (No. 69) is always
associated with him in my mind.   Many years ago,
when he happened to be in the capital, I heard him
announce this hymn at a service at Ambòhitantèly
church.   The congregation proceeded to sing it, but
when we came to the fourth verse (which speaks of
giving oneself to God to be His servant), Mr. Pearse
raised his hand and asked us to stop.   He then most
earnestly, lovingly, and solemnly urged the people to
reflect upon the words they were about to utter, and
asked them not to sing the verse unless they really
intended to yield themselves wholly to God.   To this
day I can remember the thrill that went through the
congregation, and the quiet, reverent way in which the
verse was finally sung—the speaker's words and manner
had evidently impressed many.

" Some of Mr. Pearse's books and tracts in the Malagasy
language have been blessed to many, and will doubtless
still be used of God to help and instruct the people
to whose welfare he devoted his life.   As a letter-writer
also he excelled, if I may speak from my own personal
experience ;   more than once have I been cheered,
helped and comforted by letters from him, in his own

beautiful hand-writing and language, and I have been enabled to ' thank God and take courage ' after their perusal.   Now he has ' entered into the joy of the Lord ' whom he served so faithfully here, but he will long be affectionately and gratefully remembered both by his fellow-workers, and by the Malagasy for whom he laboured during so many years."

Rev. W. E. Cousins says : " As a preacher in the Malagasy language Mr. Pearse soon had a well-recognized position.   Tall and somewhat serious in demeanour, with a good voice, and a weighty and deliberate style of utterance, his preaching made a deep impression on the minds of the people.   He never hurried, and was wont to put the same thing in various forms and to continue his illustration and enforcement of it until he felt sure the people had seized his meaning.   His sermons were always carefully planned, and his main divisions were well marked and emphasized.   They were usually stated in terse and arresting language, and the interest and attention of his people were secured.   Then by stroke upon stroke he would drive home his points.   I remember his preaching thus in the sixties, and shortly before I left Madagascar, in 1899, I heard him for the last time. The style remained substantially the same ; but of course, in the thirty years or more that had passed, his knowledge of the idioms of the language and of the character of the people had been greatly enriched.   Few came into closer daily contact with the Malagasy than he did, especially from the time he did so much medical work. He had a very intimate knowledge of the thoughts and ways of the people, and of their common sayings, and this knowledge he often used in his sermons with great skill.   I do not think I ever heard him preach in a more weighty and impressive manner than on this last occasion. He seemed to have the people fully in his grip throughout the whole service.

"In his writing for the press the same characteristics were manifested. He wrote much for *Teny Soa* and for our various publications, and also published a fair number of tracts and sermons. To these he would affix short telling titles, such as : ' Cut off thy hand. Put out thine eye'; 'Not to be bought, but freely given when asked for'; ' Mr. Loving Both Ways.'

"Perhaps his most valuable contributions were his commentaries on the two Epistles to the Corinthians, the two Epistles to the Thessalonians, and the Epistle to the Philippians. In these we see the same full and patient statement, the same aptitude in using native sayings or referring to native customs and ideas, and the same wish to make his readers fully understand the matter in hand."

Rev. H. T. Johnson writes : " It was early in 1875 that I first saw Mr. Pearse, at the London Missionary Society Mission-house in Blomfield Street. He was then preparing for returning to Madagascar, to open up a new mission in the Antsihànaka Province. The store-room at the House was full of goods ready for shipment to Madagascar, and Mr. Pearse with pocket-book in hand was seeing that all the goods for his new mission had arrived.

" The next time I saw him was six years afterwards, in September, 1881, when Mrs. Johnson and I arrived in Fìanàrantsòa from England to commence our work in Bètsilèo. We were very hospitably received by Mr. and Mrs. Pearse on that Wednesday mid-day, our first entrance into the town where we have now lived for thirty years.

" There was no house in which we could reside at

first, and so for eight months or more we shared Mr. and Mrs. Pearse's house, and not only had their friendship, but what was of immense importance to us both, we gained an experience in missionary work which has been of life-long service to us.

" Our early difficulties with the language were made much easier by being able to read Malagasy with our friends, and to be generally helped over the mysterious constructions of an eastern language. Then, too, I was especially guided in my work with the Malagasy people. I could always ask the advice of Mr. Pearse, and found his direction sane and useful. To-day I am much indebted to him for his wise counsel during those first days of a new and difficult career.

" Living with him in this town of Fìanàrantsòa during the whole time he was in the province, I was thrown much into work with him. I was constantly associated with him in the construction of buildings and it was in this department that I saw how painstaking he was in every detail and how he would never pass a piece of masonry or carpentry unless it was finished with plumb-line and straight-edge. The Malagasy workmen who came under his influence were therefore trained into doing the best and most durable work.

" During his second furlough in England I was asked by the Bètsilèo District Committee to carry on the medical work in our dispensary in Fìanàrantsòa. For a few months before Mr. Pearse's departure I went with him regularly to the dispensary, and accompanied him on his visits to the Malagasy patients in their homes, and there I saw how patient he was, and with what loving service he carried out his medical work. To this day he is remembered all over this province by

those who were so kindly and so successfully treated by
their missionary. Since those early days, medical
work has much developed, and on Mr. Pearse's return
from England, he at once set to work to construct a
small hospital and dispensary, which was further extended when Dr. G. H. Peake arrived in 1893 to carry
on, as a fully qualified doctor, the work which Mr. Pearse
had done so much to further and develop. As mission
families we cannot be too grateful to him for his loving
services to us in our homes during times of sickness.

"I am to-day the missionary in charge of the
"Antrànobirìky' church in Fìanàrantsòa, a church
built up by Mr. Pearse, and in which he laboured for
the whole of the seventeen years he was a missionary
of the London Missionary Society in this Bètsilèo
province. Here again I saw what a great missionary
he was, and how he had led the church to be strong, and
to a great extent self-supporting. His preaching,
excelled by no other missionary in Madagascar ; his
Bible-classes and personal visitation of the people have
made his name a household one, and to-day there are
many who are much to the front in Christian life and
activity, who regard Mr. Pearse's teaching as the great
impetus in their life.

" When he was engaged in writing anything for the
press, and especially the useful and important commentaries in the Malagasy language, he would often
ask me to sit in his study and hear his notes read, and
although I was but a stripling compared to him in
missionary experience, he would ask whether I could
offer any suggestions in order that his writings might
be more clearly understood by the Malagasy.

" One cannot forget his love for the garden, and
how much he did to propagate flowers and plants which

he brought either from England or from Cape Town *en route*.

"His was a strenuous life of loving and devoted service. To know him intimately as Mrs. Johnson and I did, for he lived with us for a year on the occasion of Mrs. Pearse's absence in England, is to remember a godly man of the finest type, one whose consecration and simple life has always been a source of strength to us, who are still helping to carry on the work in this part of Madagascar.

"His love for the Malagasy people was most wonderful. One may say without any reservation, that no missionary has ever lived and worked in this great African island who more devotedly lived for the people."

Others have conveyed, in a few sentences, various other striking thoughts.

Rev. T. Rowlands wrote: "He was a very rare man in many ways, an all-round missionary and a *very fine* character."

Mrs. Sibree says: "For a long time, when I visited the capital, I used always to try and hear him preach, because I said he was so clear and easy to understand."

Rev. A. S. Huckett wrote: "It is quite impossible to express the debt of gratitude we owe to him, and the Malagasy, I know, feel the same. In season and out of season he was ever ready to help others."

Mrs. Sharman wrote: "He was a born missionary, and few, if any, ever had such an influence in Madagascar. We are blessed in having known him."

Rev. C. Jukes wrote: "He was one of the most devout and useful men we ever had in the mission field; his thorough conscientiousness and his cheerful self-

sacrifice in the work of his Master were leading qualities
of his.   With all my heart I thank God that He gave
us Joseph Pearse."

The Rev. W. Evans, of Antanànarìvo, wrote : " Each
time I had the pleasure of visiting him, when home on
furlough some years ago, he invariably spoke of Antsihànaka.   When he heard of my proposed visit to the
churches there, which, together with Pastor Raini-
tiarary I paid two years ago, he wrote me a most
pathetic letter, full of loving messages and exhortations
to his old friends.   At Ambàtondrazàka there is, at
present, a well-built chapel, with a strong church ; there
are also strong churches in three other large villages.
Those of Ambàtondrazàka and Imèrimandròso will
stand favourable comparison with the best country
churches in Imèrina.   At each of these places there is
a large congregation, composed of Hova and Sihànaka,
and a well-attended Sunday school, together with
temperance and other societies.   We are now reaping
the fruit so faithfully sown by our dear friend and by the
noble band of men who succeeded him."

CHAPTER XVIII

Native Testimony

ACKNOWLEDGMENT must be made of valuable help rendered in the collection of material by many of the pastors in Antanànarìvo, and by evangelists, pastors, and teachers in other parts of the island, who knew Mr. Pearse well and had worked with him. These have sent us interesting details from their own recollection, and from inquiry made in likely quarters. The request was made to them that they would commit to writing what they could find out about Mr. Pearse's work, and the response was very hearty and full of interest. The details given have been largely incorporated in the above chapters, but there remains one account, of a more critical and elaborate character, which was given in the form of an address at the memorial gathering held at Fìanàrantsòa, which seems, both from its critical value, and from its interest as a native production, to deserve translation and reproduction *in extenso*. The writer, Rajaònimarìa by name, to whom allusion has already been made, was a teacher and evangelist under Mr. Pearse for nearly twenty years in the Bètsilèo province, and after his expulsion during the troublous times, returned to Fìanàrantsòa as pastor of one of the city churches. He writes: "I want to give from my own observation some account of Mr. Pearse's work here at Fìanàrantsòa and Sandra.

"I. His Method of Preaching.

" This I like to place in the forefront, as it is the principal part, the summing up, of all the work of the mission.

" We have seen and know that Mr. Pearse was a real messenger of God well grounded in the Word to be preached and able to apply it to the needs of all, so that whether his sermons were on the foundations of faith, or exhortations, or expositions, or narrative from which to draw warning and encouragement for the hearers, or whether they were on the parables, they were always, on every occasion, appropriate to his audience.

" We often see that though it is always the Word of God that is preached there are some points which go straight home to the hearers, while others are only understood by a few, but it appeared to me to be a characteristic of Mr. Pearse's preaching that, by his manner of preaching and arrangement of his thoughts, what he said appealed to all who listened to him. His gift in this direction is one subject for thanksgiving to God, for every time they heard him there was no disappointment among his hearers, for they all had something to be considered and from which they could learn.

" Also on account of his manner of presenting his message it was easy for the hearers to follow his line of thought from point to point. There was already something to draw the hearts of the hearers from the subjects they had been thinking of outside the church, and their interest carried them on from point to point from the beginning to the end of the sermon so that when they reached the ' Amen ' they were ready to acknowledge cheerfully and intelligently that they had taken in what Mr. Pearse had said.

" In his sermons he was most particular never to use a foreign word unless he was absolutely compelled to do so, and on such occasions he was most punctilious in explaining the meaning of such a word so that it might be comprehended by everybody. The reason of that was his anxiety that all present should understand clearly what he was saying and that those of less intelligence and less education might not be discouraged at hearing foreign words ; also he was afraid lest their thoughts might centre round such a word rather than on the spiritual food from which they were meant to receive nourishment. I myself remember being spoken to and admonished after preaching in his presence ; he called me aside and cautioned me against using such words without adding a very full explanation because, as he said, there would be many people in the church who were ignorant of its meaning, and it was better to use simple language understood by everyone so that even the dullest of comprehension could grasp it. I understood what he meant by that, and though it is nearly thirty years ago, I have carefully guarded my lips each time I have preached, so as to keep myself from using such words in case they might keep some of the weaker ones from the spiritual food from which they should have benefited.

" II. His Teaching.

" His Bible-class teaching resembled both his preaching and the commentaries of which he wrote so many. Here in Fìanàrantsòa, and in the country, it was clear and edifying, so that from the dullest to the quickest-witted all were really *taught* by it. It was easily understood, easily retained and easily remembered and also easily passed on to others.

" He was fond of illustrating his teaching by historical allusions, all the knowledge and ability that he had was used for impressing his teaching on his scholars ; everything was made clear so that it could be thoroughly grasped and he bestowed much care on the presentation of the teaching.   He had no desire to cover much ground at the expense of clearness ; he was quite satisfied to get through only two or three verses even, so long as they were thoroughly considered.   The work was conscientiously done as in the presence of God, and we often heard in his teaching, such words as these : ' If one is doing anything for God, let it be of the very best and, in the doing of it, take all the pains possible ;   hurry and dash are not befitting.   Remember that one is working in God's presence.'

" How to do good to people's souls was the great aim in his teaching. This was no light matter with him, but a deep and weighty concern. In his teaching he would always discourage the introduction of anything too abstruse, for fear of leading his scholars away from simple faith or agitating their minds. In this way anyone who tried to show off by asking what he thought profound questions was answered simply and in love, but in such a way that there was no repetition of the offence.

" Growth in grace was also what he desired for his hearers ; the grown-up people received sound teaching, the young suitable exhortation, the children good ideals to lead them to the truth, and the aged, who had accepted salvation, were urged to put to the best use the time that they had ; all these fed on his teaching, and were able to talk of the precious words that had been spoken.

" The unfolding of the spiritual teaching was his

primary object, but he touched on all kinds of practical incidents of daily life also. His teaching was thus sufficiently broad to include all that could help and do good to soul and body. This man was truly a father and mother to us!

"III. HIS HABIT ON MEETING WITH WORKERS.

" If anyone came to see him at home he had them shown into a sitting room if he happened to be engaged on anything that could not be set aside. He had them brought in because he knew that it was unpleasant for them and apt to give offence if he left them outside five, ten, twenty or thirty minutes, just waiting his leisure. If, however, he was not occupied, he himself would go to the door to show them in, a small matter, yet one that won the hearts of the Malagasy to him as to a true friend. When they were seated, they would talk together about the particular object of the visit, and his behaviour altogether was redolent of the spirit of love. If the conversation were on right lines, well and good, but if not, and anything not quite as it ought to be was mentioned, he did not say hard or cutting things, but spoke gently and gave suitable advice in such a way that no offence was taken, and both he and his visitors were able to separate with mutual regard.

" It was always a habit of his to escort his visitors outside or to the gate even, and this show of attention in itself attracted many to him.

" On meeting with fellow-workers at church there would be simple easy conversation in a spirit of love on what would help their brethren and advance the church of God. His mode of dealing with difficulties was not by over-riding the opinion of everyone else, but by trying to train his people to meet and settle their difficulties in the right way, and in this way, too, he made his helpers helpers indeed. He encouraged all his congregations to build suitable churches, so that in his district there was a large number of churches well built and provided with glass windows. He used to say, ' Your own houses, my friends, are well-finished, and as you wish them to be, but the house of God is not satisfactory ; do your best to build that well and when you see what to do, collect all the money you can for it, and come to me, and I will add an equal sum, so that we may finish the church well.' This ability to lead on the people and encourage them to do right was one of his great characteristics, but his encouragement did not take the form simply of words ; he took his share in giving freely and cheerfully as well. In this way the people were led to set to work in an enthusiastic spirit, those who could do so giving money and those who could not, giving their services. Thus the meeting would break up with gladness.

" IV. HIS DEALINGS WITH THE PEOPLE IN HIS
CHURCHES.

" He was willing to take infinite trouble over his people. When he was in the pulpit he would always take an opportunity of looking round and noticing who were there and who were absent, because he knew by name all who attended. Those who were absent he made a note of, for visiting during the week. When he was at their house he would never begin by putting leading questions to them, but talk over general matters, after the manner of the Malagasy, asking after their health, their children and so on, and when conversation had gone on he would ask them about the service, the preacher and the text on the previous Sabbath, till they had to confess that they were not there! Then would come exhortation to greater attention in the future, to diligence in prayer and following what was right and in being more regular in attendance. This method very often took effect.

" When he visited a Malagasy house, he would proceed just in the native fashion; first of all with the usual announcement of a guest demanding admission ('Haody'); this gave the people time to make a little preparation, and then they would come to the door and usher him in. He did not confine his visits to the rich, but visited all, and if the people happened to be poor, and not quite in the position to receive a guest, he tried to put them at their ease at once, telling them he was no different from themselves and sitting down wherever he could, even though there were no chair for him. If it happened to be meal time, he would give them confidence by telling them to bring out what they had to eat, that they might eat together, and then, whether it were rice, or meat or greens, manioc, sweet potato or Indian corn he would take whatever was offered. This is a sign of great intimacy among the Malagasy, for usually if they are invited to join in the meal they will excuse themselves. When the natives saw his willingness to be friends with them in such a way, it bound their hearts to him at once.

" On entering the house he would begin to talk. At first he would find some subject likely to interest his host, such as his business, whether he were a merchant, a labourer, a smith, carpenter, government servant, or handicrafts man, and they would find plenty to converse about in an easy manner. But when the talk had gone on for some time he would be sure to direct it so that he

could use the opportunity for trying to lead the people
he was visiting to serve God, and would encourage them
to do good, while time was given them.

" People in the household who could not read he would
encourage to learn, and to those who could, would be
committed the duty of teaching them. Those able to
read well would be encouraged to read the Bible diligently
and to love it. They were also enjoined to listen well
and receive the word preached to them.

"V. His Work of Healing.

" Mr. Pearse did the work of a doctor as well as all
of which we have spoken. He took that up in his desire
to further and complete the establishment of God's
kingdom in the hearts of those whom he might be able
to reach. And this work gave him opportunities, which
he could have enjoyed in no other way, of leading people
to God.

" What a work he did! With what simplicity, so
full of love and yet doing good to such hosts of sick !
His patience was wonderful. How often he was willing
to listen to the outpourings of the patient's friends in
their anxiety, and even to go with them in the night to
do what he could for some poor Malagasy. With his
stick and his lantern and a little medicine he would start
off with them at twelve or one o'clock at night, not
thinking of his own fatigue, but ready to shed grace
upon those who were needing him. A few questions,
and then the medicine would be given according to the
requirements of the case. But he did not rest satisfied
with that ; there was always an encouraging word and
the patient was pointed to the Saviour, and his heart
gladdened by such gracious attention. The mere sight
of him and the sound of his gracious words sufficed to

begin the work of restoration and soothe the pain.
After making all the arrangements necessary and
directing the friends what to do he would go off home
again all by himself. The friends would always want
to escort him but he insisted and used often to say : ' Oh,
no ! I do not mind going alone, for I am not afraid of
witches ! ' Seeing that many of those whom he went
to were scared of witches, and put down their ailments
to the power of witchcraft, he tried to gently teach
them a little lesson. He did not stop with that one
visit, for as often as need be, and especially whenever the friends asked him, he would go and do his
utmost.

" He also treated patients at his dispensary which
was open on Monday and Tuesday, Thursday and Friday,
and always, unless he had some exceedingly important
church business to settle, he was to be found there.

" His skill was wonderful, and not less so his forbearance, his endurance and his love, and these were
at the call of anyone who was in need, not merely his
favourites, but *everybody*.

"VI. HIS MANNER OF LIFE.

" There were many beautiful characteristics in his
daily life ; he was always ready to receive those who
came to him, quite simply but lovingly ; his face was
always bright and his manner pleasant, and often there
was a ready jest to put them at their ease. His manner
was always appropriate and respectful, and he was most
careful, lest he should show irritation, even though there
were things calculated to cause him displeasure ; he
was always calm and collected. I worked with him first
as a teacher in Fìanàrantsòa for eight years, and then,
for nearly twelve years, I was constantly in the way of

meeting him after I became an evangelist in his district, but in all that time I can truthfully say that not once did I ever see him cross, or irritable, or angry, or anything else than perfectly placid and master of himself.

" At the same time he held fixedly to the course he deemed to be right and suitable, and did his best to have it carried out, not by threats or anger, but judiciously ; if any one showed an inadequate conception of his responsibilities, he was well able to give the necessary admonition, and if, on the contrary, anyone seemed to have an undue sense of the importance of his position, he was suitably put in his right place ; but all so calmly and reasonably and in a way calculated to give the least offence possible.   Here is a case in point.   There were once eighteen of us attending his class, in which, for two months we were studying the subject of the resurrection, in 1 Corinthians xv.   He was most anxious to find out if we had really grasped his teaching, so he proposed an examination.   We were given a month in which to write an essay ;   at the end of that time we gave in what we had written and he told us that, on account of his wish to adjudicate fairly and without haste, he would take a fortnight over his corrections and then call us again. When we returned to him he expressed his pleasure at all the papers written, and said that, though all were good, there were two which were decidedly better than the rest, and to those he awarded the prizes.   There was one of the class, however, who objected, and said that his paper was quite as good as those awarded the prizes and he had spent as much pains over it as did the other two men, and Mr. Pearse's judgment was partial and unsound and influenced by favouritism. He quite lost his temper, and gave himself away altogether, and insulted Mr. Pearse beyond endurance.

We reasoned with him, and besought him to be quiet, and finally led him out. But what about Mr. Pearse? No anger, no rage, no loss of his own self-control; he calmly and smilingly praised the lad for his paper, but re-affirmed his award, and besought him to accept the situation reasonably. We were astonished beyond measure at this forbearance; almost anyone else would have spoken sharply and many would have used language that might have left incurable wounds, but he! no, the right spirit shown even under the greatest provocation. That was a lesson learnt from the Master, and I have had many an occasion to look back upon it and take it to myself.

" Another characteristic was that he did not seem to have any favourites, but to all, whether his own congregation or no, whether Christians or no, if he was able to do them good, he did it.

" VII. His Encouragement of Faithful Workers.

" He was accustomed to judge the work of others not by its general effect, but in detail, and wherever he found good work, whether from those associated with him in church work, or those to whom he entrusted things he wanted made, or his personal bearers and attendants even, he regarded such people as real friends. His servants he used to meet with morning and evening for instruction in reading and for prayer. Two great objects he always kept in view with regard to those about him— how to do good to their souls and to their bodies. His help to his friends was shown in many ways; his sound advice, his beneficial teaching, his sympathy with the distressed, his help to those in perplexity, were all examples of his giving of himself for others.

"VIII. His Avoidance of Gossip.

" There are always people who talk ; some tell the truth, some tell tales in order to curry favour ; some spy upon others out of ill-will and spite. This brings great difficulties upon the mission, and is very difficult to deal with. Sometimes the good have been dropped upon and the bad have been unduly raised up.

" But Mr. Pearse was never influenced by such recitals, he had his own judgment of people, and did not allow himself to be carried away by gossip and tale-telling. Everything was duly weighed, and everything was perfectly ordered.

"IX. His Bearing towards Outsiders.

" He showed himself all things to all men if by any means he might save some. Some of those who were simple and ignorant, whom he dealt with simply, became workers in his churches. Whenever he went into the country he always made a point of trying to have a talk with the people in the house at which he happened to be staying, and he would not rest nor take his meal until he had been able to try and help them. When he reached his churches he would wander away to the surrounding houses, especially to those occupied by people whom he had heard of as difficult to influence, and by his loving spirit he was able to bring many of these to the truth. Where he heard of anyone who had baffled the attempts of others to win him, there would he make a point of going so as to deal with them individually and personally. He was not content with his preaching, nor his teaching, nor his healing the sick, nor with the mere presentation of the truth, but he went out himself to *seek* those who were outside and difficult of reach.

And what he did, he did thoroughly and with a will.
Truly he was a man who really loved the Malagasy,
and his life and work, his efforts and endeavours all
abundantly prove this.   We have had many friends, of
very different nationalities, but Mr. Pearse was one
among a thousand.   'May my death be that of the
righteous and may my last end be like his.' "